Noa Noa

Noa Noa

Gauguin's Tahiti

edited and introduced by
Nicholas Wadley

translated by Jonathan Griffin

Phaidon · Oxford

This edition first published in 1985 by
Phaidon Press Limited
Littlegate House, St Ebbe's Street, Oxford OX1 1SQ

This edition ©1985 by John Calmann and Cooper Ltd
71 Gt Russell Street, London WC1B 3BN

Translation by arrangement with Bruno Cassirer Ltd

British Library Cataloguing in Publication Data

Gauguin, Paul
    Noa Noa: Gauguin's Tahiti.
    1. Gauguin, Paul,   2. Painters—France
    —Biography
    I. Title
    759.4   ND553.G27

    ISBN 0-7148-2375-9

This book was designed and produced by
John Calmann and Cooper Ltd, London

Filmset by Composing Operations Ltd, Tunbridge Wells, Kent
Printed in Hong Kong by Mandarin Offset Ltd

1 Frontispiece: *Noa Noa* (Fragrant). *c.* 1894. Woodcut, 35 × 20 cm. Guérin 17. Museum of Modern
Art, New York (Lillie P. Bliss Coll.)

Contents

Introduction

Gauguin wrote intermittently throughout his working life as an artist: articles, manuscripts, letters, notes. He saw writing as an inferior medium to painting and even felt it necessary to insist that he was not a writer. Nevertheless, he acknowledged that the pen could say things that should not be expected of the brush and most of his manuscripts bear an explicitly complementary relationship to his art. His writing is as uninhibited, as unabashed in its plundering of available sources and as abrupt and empirical in its various manners as his visual imagery. *Noa Noa* was his most substantial undertaking in words and the only text that he unequivocally intended for publication as a book.

In 1883, at the age of thirty-four, he had abandoned a relatively successful bourgeois life to become a painter. Eight difficult and uneven years followed in which he tried to establish himself as an artist. When, in 1891, he made another momentous decision – to abandon Europe for Tahiti – he already enjoyed considerable standing among younger artists and writers as one of the most radical leaders of the Symbolist movement in France. His return to Paris after only two years in Tahiti was open to interpretation as either triumph or capitulation. For Gauguin it was a risk, a trial of strength and confidence. The idea of *Noa Noa* was born out of the doubts and certainties which accompanied his reunion with Europe. While, on the face of it, the book is a simple account of his first two years in Tahiti, it can more fruitfully be seen as an exposition and justification of his position as a mature artist.

The final outcome of the project satisfied no one and circumstances surrounding *Noa Noa*'s evolution have made it the subject of much subsequent confusion and misunderstanding, not least because there exist three principal and distinct versions of the text. These are:

1. *DRAFT MS* of 1893
This first manuscript, which forms the text of this volume, was Gauguin's original draft for *Noa Noa*: eleven short sections of text, mostly narrative, much of it in incomplete or note form.

2. *LOUVRE MS* of 1893/7
This manuscript is also in Gauguin's hand. It represents an enlarged version of the original text as redrafted by Gauguin's collaborator, the poet Charles Morice (1861–1919), in close consultation with Gauguin, *c.* 1893–4. Some new text by Morice was incorporated at the time and a few further Morice poems were copied into the MS later by Gauguin, in 1897. Gauguin's illustrations were partly made when he first copied out the text, but the majority were added some time later, back in Tahiti.

3. *'LA PLUME' EDITION* of 1901
This is the definitive printed version, alone in incorporating the full texts by both Gauguin and Morice and, apart from excerpts that appeared in *La Revue Blanche* in 1897, the only published edition to carry the names of both writers.

2 Still life (after Delacroix). 1894/7. Watercolour, 17 × 12 cm. Frontispiece of the Louvre MS

As this sequence indicates, the book was conceived as an unusual form of collaboration between the painter and a professional writer. Gauguin and Morice did not set out to write a joint text, but to work as co-authors contributing interleaved chapters: alternately narration by Gauguin and poetry by Morice, or – as their later preface puts it – the memory of the painter and the imagination of the poet.

Gauguin explained the purpose of the book in terms of making his Tahitian paintings better understood. The collaboration was to facilitate this by creating an illuminating contrast between the primitive consciousness (his own) and that of the cultured European (Morice's). Much of the subsequent criticism of their collaboration – already being voiced in Gauguin's lifetime – ignores this intention entirely. Morice has been dismissed as an ambitious entrepreneur whose trivial poems have dragged down the positive clarity of Gauguin's vision. In his first manuscript, all the qualities that Gauguin brought to the book are immediately present – his naïve romanticism, acute perceptions, prodigal imagination and disarmingly erratic literary abilities. That these qualities were subsequently (and inevitably) tempered by Morice's contribution as the book took shape has been deplored by successive biographers and historians. That Gauguin was a very willing party to the collaboration and that – to start with at least – he clearly expected professional editorial advice and help from Morice: all of this has been conveniently played down.

The prejudice against Morice has been fortuitously compounded by the fact that the three major versions of the text identified above were published in reverse order. The first Noa Noa to be published was the *La Plume* edition of 1901. The Louvre MS was published for the first time in 1924. The Draft MS, the very earliest surviving script of Noa Noa, was first published in 1954. The effect of this reversal is that public knowledge of Noa Noa has moved successively from the intended final form of the book, combining complete texts by both authors; through an intermediate state containing all of Gauguin's texts as edited by Morice, but only an incomplete form of Morice's own contribution; to, finally, Gauguin's own first draft for the book, virtually untouched by Morice.

At the second and third publications, the most partisan of Gauguin commentators each time welcomed what they saw as a further erosion of Morice's undesirable interference. The Draft MS, which Gauguin hurriedly wrote for Morice to work from in 1893, has been hailed rather misleadingly as the only true version of Noa Noa. With its proper role in the history of Noa Noa thus disguised, the character of the Draft MS – not least its improvisatory fragmentariness and moments of discontinuity – is easily misunderstood.

Almost as much misguided controversy has surrounded the content of the book. At first encounter, Gauguin's contributions to Noa Noa have every appearance of an autobiographical account of his first stay in Tahiti. They appear to describe the places, people and events that framed his life there, in a narrative sequence. The evidence that has unfolded steadily since Gauguin's death tells a different story. We now know that he adapted the facts around him to fit his dream; that this is an evocation of Tahiti more than a description. Not only did he invent some of his 'truths', but he borrowed many others word for word from a single source and, furthermore, he chose not to distinguish that borrowed material from his own experience. All of this has prompted accusations of deceit, fraudulence and plagiarism.

In reality, of course, questions of truth or falsehood are not relevant. One might almost as well condemn Matisse's *Joie de Vivre* as 'inaccurate' or Baudelaire's *Invitation au Voyage* as 'false'. If the mood of the late nineteenth century, with its dreams of a Golden Age, were not enough to warn against such inappropriate questions, then the very essence of Gauguin's own art should have done so. The Paradise that he dreamt of no longer existed – probably never had – and, outside of his art, he made no serious attempt to conceal this. Tahiti was the symbol of an ideal for him: his picture of it was neither true nor false.

In relation to the Gauguin legend, *Noa Noa* stands as both confirmation and corrective. It exemplifies the romantic visions of escape that have fostered the legend, as well as the degree to which his perception of reality was formed and coloured by them. On the other hand – and most clearly of all in the Draft MS – it also gives glimpses of the hesitations, mistakes, false starts and loneliness that attended this first confrontation of his dream.

Noa Noa is autobiographical in character, but it is at the same time essentially an imaginative work, dealing freely in invented and/or ready-made images. Its main sources are Gauguin's own experience and Maori myth and legend. These are woven into an evocative narrative form, which meanders between external reality, symbol and emotive fantasy. In these senses *Noa Noa*, more than all Gauguin's other writings, is an exact literary counterpart to his painted and carved images.

In this first annotated English edition, I have endeavoured to make Gauguin's Draft MS more accessible in two ways. One is to set the manuscript in the context of his art and writing as a whole. The other is to draw detailed comparisons with the Louvre Manuscript, the only version of *Noa Noa* in which Gauguin was actively involved, as means to a better understanding of his intention. Three additional narrative episodes from the Louvre MS are included here as an appendix to Gauguin's draft. The first versions of these must have formed part of Gauguin's original material for *Noa Noa*, dating from the same period as the Draft MS. They belong with it and I have translated and included them here for that reason.

The translation of the MS is that of Jonathan Griffin. When it was first published in 1961, he wrote that as translator 'one tries to keep out of the way' in order to preserve 'its sketch form, jerky directness, authentic freshness'. Apart from a few corrections, his 1961 translation is preserved intact, including the division into eleven 'chapters'. These have been questioned by Jean Loize, the sole important pioneer of *Noa Noa* studies (1961, 1966). However, there are clear enough indications in the margins of Gauguin's manuscript to justify their retention. The correspondence between these 'chapters' and the chapters of the Louvre MS is given on pp. 150–1.

In the captions to the plates, the 'W' catalogue numbers refer to Wildenstein 1964; the 'Gray' numbers to Gray 1963 and the 'Guérin' numbers to Guérin 1927. Full details of these titles are given in the bibliography on pp. 154–5. All paintings are in oil on canvas unless otherwise stated.

Nicholas Wadley

3 *Ta Matete* (We shall not go to market today). s. & d. 1892. 73 × 92 cm. W476.
Kunstmuseum, Basel

Noa Noa

Gauguin's original manuscript

I

1 For 63 days I have been on my way, and I burn to reach the longed-for land. On
2 June 8th we saw strange fires moving about in zig-zags – fishermen. Against a
3 dark sky a jagged black cone stood out. We were rounding Moorea and coming
in sight of Tahiti. A few hours later the dawn twilight became visible, and slowly
we approached the reefs of Tahiti, then entered the fairway and anchored
4 without mishap in the roads. To a man who has travelled a good deal this small
island is not, like the bay of Rio Janeiro, a magic sight. A few peaks of
sub[merged] mountain [were left] after the Deluge; a family climbed up there,
took root, the corals also climbed, they ringed round the new island.
5   At ten in the morning I called on Governor Lacascade, who received me as
6 a man of consequence entrusted by the Government with a mission – ostensibly
artistic but mainly consisting in political spying. I did all I could to undeceive the
political people, it was no good. They thought I was paid, I assured them I was
not.
     At that time the king was fatally ill, and every day an end was expected. The
town had a strange look: on the one hand the Europeans – traders, officials,
officers and soldiers – continued to laugh [and] sing in the streets, while the
natives assumed grave expressions [and] gossiped in low voices around the
palace.
     And in the roadstead an unusual stir of boats with orange sails, upon the blue
sea frequently crossed by the silvered ripples from the line of the reefs. The
inhabitants of the neighbouring islands were coming in, each day, to be present
at their king's last moment, at the final taking-over of their islands by the
7 French. For their voices from on high brought them warning – (every time a king
is dying, their mountains, they say, have sombre patches on some of their slopes
at sunset).
8   The king died and lay in state in his palace, in the full-dress uniform of an
admiral.
9   There I saw the queen – Marau was her name – decorating the royal room
with flowers and draperies. When the director of public works asked my advice
about arranging the apartment artistically, I signed to him to look at the queen
as, with the fine instinct of the Maoris, she gracefully adorned and turned
everything she touched into a work of art.
     'Leave it to them,' I replied.
     Having only just arrived, rather disappointed as I was by things being so far
from what I had longed for and (this was the point) imagined, disgusted as I was

by all this European triviality, I was in some ways blind. And so I saw in the already aging queen a stout ordinary woman with some remnants of beauty. That day the Jewish element in her blood had absorbed all else. I was strangely wrong. When I saw her again later, I understood her Maori charm; the Tahitian blood began to get the upper hand once more, the remembrance of her ancestor the great chieftain Tati conferred on her, on her brother, on the whole of that family in general, a real impressiveness. In her eyes, a sort of vague presentiment 10 of those passions which shoot up in an instant – an island rising from the Ocean and the plants beginning to burgeon in the first sunshine.

For two days the singing of *hyménées* – choruses. Everyone in black. Dirges. I thought I heard Beethoven's *Sonate pathétique*.

Funeral of Pomaré. – 6 o'clock, the cortège leaves the palace. The troops . . . the authorities . . . black clothes white helmets. All the districts marched in order, and each with its chief bearing the French flag. Great mass of black—— So [they went] till [they reached] the part called Arne. A monument there, indescribable in its contrast with the beautiful scenery. A formless heap of coral lumps bound together with cement. Speech by Lacascade – usual cliché – translated afterwards by the interpreter. Speech by the Protestant Pastor, then a reply by Tati, the queen's brother.

That was all – Carriages into which the officials piled, as though returning from the races——

Along the road, confusion. The indifference of the French set the example, and all this people, so grave during the last few days, began laughing again; *vahines* once more took their *tanes* by the arm, wagging their buttocks, while their broad bare feet ponderously trampled the dust of the roadway. Arrived near the Fatana river, a general scattering. In some places women, hiding among the stones, crouched in the water with their skirts raised to the girdle, cleansing their thighs of the soiling dust from the road, [and] cooling their knees which the march and the heat had chafed. Thus restored they again took the road for Papeete, their breasts leading and the conical shells which tipped their nipples drawing the muslin of their dresses to a point, with all the suppleness and grace 11 of a healthy animal, and spreading round about them that mixture of animal scent and of sandalwood and gardenias. '*Teine merahi Noa Noa* (now very 12 fragrant),' they said.

That was all – everything went back to normal. There was one king less, and with him were vanishing the last vestiges of Maori customs. It was all over – 13 nothing but civilized people left.

I was sad, coming so far to. 14
. . . .
Shall I manage to recover any trace of that past, so remote and so mysterious? and the present had nothing worthwhile to say to me. To get back to the ancient hearth, revive the fire in the midst of all these ashes. And, for that, quite alone, without any support. 15

Cast down though I am, I am not in the habit of giving up without having

4 Above: *L'Univers est Créé* (The universe was created). *c.*1894/5. Woodcut, 20.5 × 35.5 cm. Guérin 25-6. Nationalmuseum, Stockholm

5 Opposite: *Man with an Axe.* s. & d. 1891. 92 × 69 cm. W430. Coll. Mr and Mrs Alexander M. Lewyt, New York

tried everything, the impossible as well as the possible. My mind was soon made up. To leave Papeete as quickly as I could, to get away from the European centre. I had a sort of vague presentiment that, by living wholly in the bush with natives of Tahiti, I would manage with patience to overcome these people's mistrust, and that I would Know.

An officer of the *gendarmerie* graciously offered me his carriage and his horse. I left, one morning, in search of my hut.

My *vahine* went with me (Titi was her name) – almost an English girl but she spoke a little French. That day she had put on her best dress, a flower behind her ear, – and her sugarcane hat, which she had plaited, was adorned, above its ribbon of straw flowers, with a trimming of orange-coloured shells. Her black hair hung loose over her shoulders; like this she looked really pretty——. She was proud of being in a carriage, she was proud of being well-dressed, she was proud of being the *vahine* of a man she believed to be important and highly paid. All this pride had nothing absurd about it, so well adapted is their cast of features for wearing dignity. Ancient memories of great chieftains (a race that has had such a feudal past)——

I well knew that all her mercenary love was composed merely of things that, in our European eyes, make a *whore*, but to one observer there was more than this. Such eyes and such a mouth could not lie.

16

There is, in all of them, a love so innate that, whether mercenary or not mercenary, it is still Love.

17 Besides I w——

In short, the journey passed pretty quickly – a little insignificant conversation, and scenery that was rich all the time but not very varied. Always to the right the sea, the coral reefs, and expanses of water which sometimes rose in smoke when the encounter with the rocks was too violent.

At noon we reached the 45th kilometre – the Mataiea district.
I visited the district and in the end found rather a fine hut, which the owner consented to let to me; he would build another next door, to live in.
On our way back, next day in the evening, Titi asked me if I would agree to take
18 her with me. 'Later, in a few days, when I've moved in.'
19 I realized that this half-white girl, glossy from contact with all those Europeans, would not fulfil the aim I had set before me. 'I shall find them by the dozen,' I said to myself. But the country is not the town.
20 And besides, is it necessary to *take them* in the Maori fashion *(Mau Saisis)*?
And I did not know their languages.

The few young girls of Mataiea who do not live with a *tane* (man) look at you with such frankness, [such] utterly fearless dignity, that I was really intimidated.
21 Also, it was said that many of them were sick. Of that sickness which the civilized Europeans have brought them in return for their generous hospitality. After a little while I let Titi know that I would be happy if she would return. And yet in Papeete she had a terrible reputation. She had buried several lovers in
22 succession.

II

Description [of] landscape – Shore side – Picture of the woodcutter——. Inland. The mango seen against the mountain, over the entrance to the impressive
23 cave——
24   I went, that evening, to smoke a cigarette on the sands by the sea-shore. The sun was rapidly approaching the horizon, was beginning to hide behind the Isle of Moorea, which I had on my right. Against its light the mountains stood out in strong black upon the blazing sky, all those crests like ancient battlemented castles. While all those lands crumble in the deluge, there still remains, respected by these waves (rumour of some immense crowd) – there still remains, of a whole feudal society that has vanished for ever, the protecting Crest – that one nearest the sky, looking down at the deep waters, and majestically (though its cleft has an ironical look) pitying, maybe, the multitude [that has been] engulfed
25 for having touched the tree of knowledge that attacks the head. Sphinx.

6 Above left: Crested head. *c.*1893. Pen and ink, 3.5 × 3.5 cm. Draft MS, supplement to p. 7
7 Above right: 'Taoa'. *c.*1891/3. Pen and ink over pencil, 10.5 × 7.5 cm. Carnet de Tahiti, p. 43

Night came quickly. This time again, Moorea was asleep. I fell asleep, later, in my bed. Silence of a Tahitian night.   26

Only the beating of my heart could be heard. The reeds of my hut in their spaced rows were visible from my bed with the moonlight filtering through them like an instrument of music. Pipo our ancestors called it, Vivo is their name for it. But silent (it speaks at night through memories). I fell asleep to that music. Above me, the great high roof of screw-pine leaves, – the lizards dwell there. In my sleep I could imagine space above my head, the vault of heaven, not a prison in which one stifles. My hut was Space, Freedom.

Near my hut there was another hut (*Fare amu*, house to eat in). Nearby, a pirogue – while the diseased coconut-palm looked like a huge parrot, with its golden tail drooping and a huge bunch of coconuts grasped in its claws——

The nearly naked man was wielding with both hands a heavy axe that left, at   27 the top of the stroke, its blue imprint on the silvery sky and, as it came down, its incision on the dead tree, which would instantly live once more a moment of flames – age-old heat, treasured up each day. On the ground purple with long serpentine copper-coloured leaves, [there lay] a whole Oriental vocabulary – letters (it seemed to me) of an unknown, mysterious language. I seemed to see that word, of Oceanic origin: *Atua*, God. As *Taäta* or *Takata* it reached India   28 and is to be found everywhere or in everything – (Religion of Buddha) – In the eyes of Tathagata all the fullest magnificence of Kings and of their ministers are merely like spittle and dust;

8 Opposite: *Vahine no te Tiare* (Woman with a flower). s. & d. 1891. 70 × 46 cm. W420. Ny Carlsberg Glyptotek, Copenhagen

9 Above: *Te Raau Rahi* (The big tree). s. & d. 1891. 71.5 × 91.5 cm. W437. Cleveland Museum of Art

In his eyes purity and impurity are like the dance of the six *nagas*.
In his eyes the search for the way of Buddha is like flowers set before a man's eyes.
    A woman was stowing some nets in the pirogue, and the horizon of the blue sea was often broken by the green of the waves' crests against the coral breakers——

    I was truly alone there, we observed one another. After two days I had exhausted my provisions, I had imagined that with money I would find all that is necessary for nourishment. The food is there, certainly, on the trees, on the mountain-slopes, in the sea, but one has to be able to climb a high tree, to go up the mountain and come back laden with heavy burdens; to be able to catch fish

[or] dive and tear from the sea-bottom the shells firmly attached to the rocks. So there I was, a civilized man, for the time being definitely inferior to the savage, and as, on an empty stomach, I was pondering sadly on my situation, a native made signs to me and shouted, in his language, 'come and eat'. I understood. But I was ashamed and, shaking my head, refused. A few minutes later a child silently laid at the side of my door some food cleanly done up in freshly picked leaves, then withdrew. I was hungry, so silently I accepted. A little later the man went by and with a kindly expression, without stopping, said to me a single word: *'Paia.'* I understood vaguely. 'Are you satisfied?'

On the ground under some clusters of broad pumpkin leaves I caught sight of a small dark head with quiet eyes.

A little child was examining me, then made off timorously when its eyes met mine. . . . These black people, these cannibal teeth, brought the word 'savages' into my mouth.

For them, too, I was the savage. Rightly perhaps.

I began to work – notes, sketches of all kinds. Everything in the landscape blinded me, dazzled me. Coming from Europe I was constantly uncertain of some colour [and kept] beating about the bush: and yet it was so simple to put naturally on to my canvas a red and a blue. In the brooks, forms of gold 30 enchanted me – Why did I hesitate to pour that gold and all that rejoicing of the sunshine on to my canvas? Old habits from Europe, probably, – all this timidity of expression [characteristic] of our bastardized races——

To initiate myself properly into the character of a Tahitian face, into all the charm of a Maori smile, I had long wanted to make a portrait of a woman who lived close by, who was of true Tahitian descent.

I asked her permission one day when she had plucked up the courage to come 31 into my hut and look at some photographs of paintings. While she was examining with a great deal of interest some religious pictures by the Italian 32 primitives, I tried to sketch some of her features, especially that enigmatic smile of hers. She made a nasty grimace, went away, – then she came back. Was it an inner struggle, or caprice (a very Maori trait), or even an impulse of coquetry that will surrender only after resistance? I realized that in my painter's scrutiny there was a sort of tacit demand for surrender, surrender for ever without any chance to withdraw, a perspicacious probing of what was within. [She was,] in fact, not pretty by European standards: Beautiful all the same – all her features had a raphaelesque harmony in their meeting curves, while her mouth, modelled by a sculptor, spoke all the tongues of speech and of the kiss, of joy and of suffering; that melancholy of the bitterness that mingles with pleasure, of passivity dwelling within domination. An entire fear of the unknown.

I worked fast, with passion. It was a portrait resembling what my eyes *veiled by my heart* perceived. I believe it was chiefly faithful to what was within. That sturdy fire from a contained strength. She had a flower behind her ear, which was listening for her fragrance. And her forehead in its majesty recalled, with its 33 raised lines, that phrase of Poe's: 'There is no perfect beauty without a cer——'

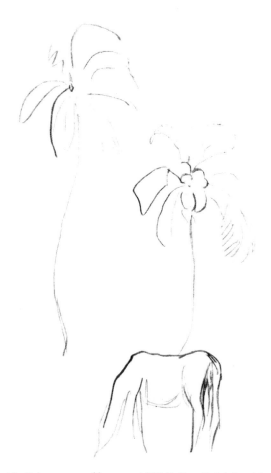

10 Palm trees and horse. *c.*1891/3. Pencil, 16.5 × 11 cm. Carnet de Tahiti, p. 39

She looked with particular interest at a photograph of Manet's Olympia. With the words I had already learned in that language (for two months I had not spoken a word of French) I questioned her. She told me this Olympia was truly beautiful: I smiled at that opinion and was moved by it. She had the sense of the beautiful (and the Ecole des Beaux Arts considers that [picture] horrible!). She added, all of a sudden, breaking the silence that presides over a thought: 'It's your wife.'

'Yes,' I lied. Me, the *tane* of Olympia!

I asked if I might paint her portrait. '*Aita* (no),' she said in a tone almost of rage, and went away.

This refusal really depressed me.

An hour later she came back in a beautiful dress – Caprice, desire for the forbidden fruit – She smelled good she was [all] adorned and I worked with haste – I suspected that this decision [of hers] was not firm – Portrait of a woman *Vahine no te tiare* ——

11 Opposite: *Tahitian Village*. s. & d. 1892. 90 × 70 cm. W480. Ny Carlsberg Glyptotek, Copenhagen

12 Above: Illustration to the woodcutting expedition. *c.*1894/5. Pen and watercolour, 9.5 × 19.5 cm. Louvre MS, p. 79

A period of work — Alone. I saw plenty of calm-eyed young women, I wanted them to be willing to be taken without a word: taken brutally. In a way a longing to rape. The old men said to me, speaking of one of them: '*Mau tera* (take this one).' I was timid and dared not resign myself to the effort—— 36

I let Titi know that I wanted her to come. She came. But being already civilized, used to an official's luxury, she did not suit me for long. I parted from her. 37

III

Alone again. . . . I became, each day, a little more savage – my neighbours were almost my friends – dressed like them, fed like them. In the evening I would go to the house where the natives from round about met. There, after an old man had carefully said a prayer and all had joined in the responses, the songs would begin. Strange music without instruments. In the intervals funny stories or wise sayings. One of these astonished me. The old man said: 'In our village you see, here and there, houses falling to ruin, rotting roofs gaping, letting the water through when it happens to rain. Why? Everyone has a right to be sheltered. There's no lack of wood, of leaves for the roof. I ask that large houses be built

23

13 *Te Fare Hymenee* (The House of Song). s. & d. 1892. 50 × 90 cm. W477.
Baltimore Museum of Art

afresh to replace those; everyone *in succession* will lend a hand (Union makes strength).' And everyone without exception applauded.

'That is good. Carried unanimously.'

I went to bed that evening full of admiration for that wise people, and next day I looked for the start of work on these houses. Nobody any longer gave it a thought. I questioned one or two people. No answer, except a few significant grins on broad dreamy faces——

It is a long way between the cup and the lips – And why that work? Have not the Gods given us every day our subsistence? The sun every day rises serene – Tomorrow – Perhaps, don't know. Is this frivolity, carelessness? . . . Or, when you think it over, philosophy? Don't get a taste for luxury, etc. . . . I withdrew.

38 Pangloss – Everything is for the best in the best of [all possible] worlds——

IV

39 Every day gets better for me, in the end I understand the language quite well, my neighbours (three close by, the others at various distances) regard me almost as

40 one of themselves; my naked feet, from daily contact with the rock, have got used to the ground; my body, almost always naked, no longer fears the sun;

civilization leaves me bit by bit and I begin to think simply, to have only a little hatred for my neighbour, and I function in an animal way, freely – with the certainty of the morrow [being] like today; every morning the sun rises serene for me as for everyone, I become carefree and calm and loving. I have a natural friend, who has come to see me every day naturally, without any interested motive. My paintings in colour [and] my wood-carvings astonished him and my answers to his questions taught him something. Not a day when I work but he comes to watch me. One day when, handing him my tools, I asked him to try a sculpture, he gazed at me in amazement and said to me simply, with sincerity, that I was not like other men; and he was perhaps the first of my fellows to tell me that I was useful to others. A child. . . . One has to be, to think that an artist is something useful.

The young man was faultlessly handsome and we were great friends. Sometimes in the evening, when I was resting from my day's work, he would ask me the questions of a young savage who wants to know a lot of things about love in Europe, questions which often embarrassed me.

One day I wished to have for sculpture a tree of rosewood, a piece of considerable size and not hollow. 'For that,' he told me, 'you must go up the mountain to a certain place where I know several fine trees that might satisfy you. If you like, I'll take you there and we'll carry it back, the two of us.'

We left in the early morning.

The Indian paths in Tahiti are quite difficult for a European: between two unscalable mountains there is a cleft where the water purifies itself by twisting between detached boulders, rolled down, left at rest, then caught up again on a torrent day to be rolled down further, and so on to the sea. On either side of the stream there cascades a semblance of a path: trees pell-mell, monster ferns, all sorts of vegetation growing wilder, more and more impenetrable as you climb towards the centre of the island.

We went naked, both of us, except for the loincloth, and axe in hand, crossing the river many a time to take advantage of a bit of track which my companion seemed to smell out, so little visible [it was], so deeply shaded. – Complete silence, – only the noise of water crying against rock, monotonous as the silence. And two we certainly were, two friends, he a quite young man and I almost an old man in body and soul, in civilized vices: in lost illusions. His lithe animal body had graceful contours, he walked in front of me sexless. . . .

From all this youth, from this perfect harmony with the nature which surrounded us, there emanated a beauty, a fragrance *(noa noa)* that enchanted my artist soul. From this friendship so well cemented by the mutual attraction between simple and composite, love took power to blossom in me.

And we were only . . . the two of us——

I had a sort of presentiment of crime, the desire for the unknown, the awakening of evil – Then weariness of the male role, having always to be strong, protective; shoulders that are a heavy load. To be for a minute the weak being who loves and obeys.

41

42

14 Above: *Pape Moë* (Mysterious water). s. & d. 1893. 99 × 75 cm. W498.
Bührle Collection, Zürich

15 Opposite top: Landscape. *c.*1896/7? Watercolour, 19.5 × 28 cm. Louvre MS, p. 183

16 Opposite bottom: *Manao Tupapau* (The spirit of the dead watches/She thinks of the spirit of the
dead). s. & d. 1892. 73 × 92 cm. W457. Albright-Knox Art Gallery, Buffalo

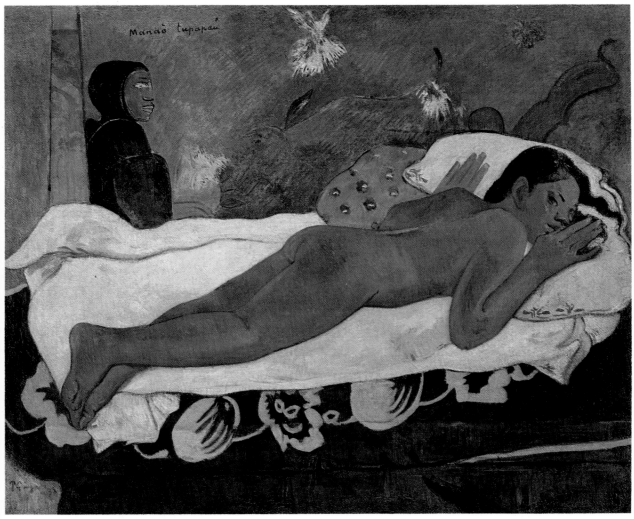

I drew close, without fear of laws, my temples throbbing.

The path had come to an end . . . we had to cross the river; my companion turned at that moment, so that his chest was towards me. The hermaphrodite had vanished; it was a young man, after all; his innocent eyes resembled the limpidity of the water. Calm suddenly came back into my soul, and this time I enjoyed the coolness of the stream deliciously, plunging into it with delight – 'Toe toe,' he said to me ('it's cold'). 'Oh no,' I answered, and this denial, answering my previous desire, drove in among the cliffs like an echo. Fiercely I thrust my way with energy into the thicket, [which had] become more and more wild; the boy went on his way, still limpid-eyed. He had not understood. I alone carried the burden of an evil thought, a whole civilization had been before me in evil and had educated me.

We were reaching our destination. – At that point the crags of the mountain drew apart, and behind a curtain of tangled trees a semblance of a plateau [lay] hidden but not unknown. There several trees (rose-wood) extended their huge branches. Savages both of us, we attacked with the axe a magnificent tree which had to be destroyed to get a branch suitable to my desires. I struck furiously and, my hands covered with blood, hacked away with the pleasure of sating one's brutality and of destroying something. In time with the noise of the axe I sang:

'Cut down by the foot the whole forest (of desires)
Cut down in yourself the love of yourself, as a man
would cut down with his hand in autumn the Lotus.'

Well and truly destroyed indeed, all the old remnant of civilized man in me. I returned at peace, feeling myself thenceforward a different man, a Maori. The two of us carried our heavy load cheerfully, and I could again admire, in front of me, the graceful curves of my young friend – and calmly: curves robust like the tree we were carrying. The tree smelt of roses, Noa Noa. We got back in the afternoon, tired. He said to me: 'Are you pleased?' 'Yes' – and inside myself I repeated: 'Yes.'

I was definitely at peace from then on.

I gave not a single blow of the chisel to that piece of wood without having memories of a sweet quietude, a fragrance, a victory and a rejuvenation.

V

By the valley of the Punaru, the island's great fissure, you reach the Tamanou plateau. From there you can see the Diadem, Orohena and Arorai. The Centre of the Island. Many people had spoken to me of it and I had conceived the plan of spending some days there alone. 'But what will you do at night? you'll be tormented by the *tupapau*. You must be mad or [at least] reckless to go and

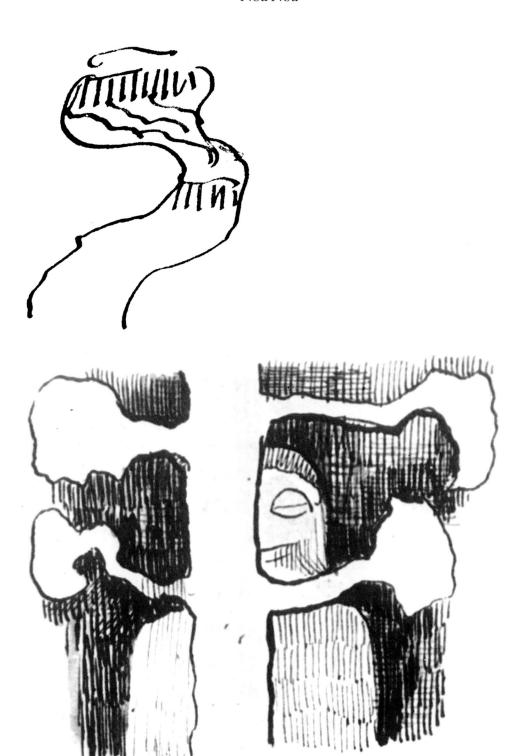

17 Top: River. *c*.1893. Pen and ink, 3 × 2.5 cm. Draft MS, p. 16

18 Above: Maori spirit. *c*.1894/5. Pen and watercolour, 5 × 6 cm. Louvre MS, p. 73

19 Top: Illustration to 'Birth of the Stars'. *c.*1892. Pen and watercolour, 10 × 16 cm. Ancien Culte Mahorie MS, p. 42

20 Illustration to the legend of Rouahatou. *c.*1892. Pen and watercolour, 7 × 15 cm. Ancien Culte Mahorie MS, p. 36

21 Above left: Illustration to 'Birth of the Stars'. c.1892. Pen and watercolour, 15 × 16 cm. Ancien Culte Mahorie MS, p. 40

22 Above right: Sailing boat. c.1896/7. Pen and watercolour, 17 × 12 cm. Louvre MS, p. 187

disturb the spirits of the mountains.' All this was just what was needed to excite my curiosity.

And so, one fine morning, I set out. For nearly two hours I followed a path along one bank of the Punaru; then I crossed the stream again and again. On either side the walls became more and more steep, enormous rocks in the stream; I had to continue my journey almost all the time in the river, with the water sometimes up to my knees, sometimes to my shoulders.

Between two excessively high walls the sunshine hardly thrust in at all. The sky blue – you could almost see the stars in full daytime. 9 o'clock. The daylight was failing and I began at last to wonder where I should spend the night, when I noticed, to one side, an acre or two of nearly flat ground where bracken, wild banana-trees and bouraos [grew] pell-mell. Luckily some ripe bananas. Hastily I made a fire – baked bananas my meal – and I settled down as best I could at the foot of a tree whose branches, across which I had entwined some banana-leaves, would give me shelter if it rained. I was cold; I was soaked from wading all day in cold water; I slept badly. I was afraid wild boar might come and take the skin off my legs, so I had slipped the cord of my axe over my wrist. Black night, impossible to see. Close to my head a [sort of] phosphorescent dust intrigued me, and I smiled as I thought of those kind Maoris who had told me beforehand those stories of the *tupapau*. I found out later that this luminous dust was a small mushroom that grows in the damp places on dead branches like the ones which had served me for my fire.

Next day at dawn I left and continued on my way.

Wilder and wilder, the river turned more and more to rapids, twisting more and more. Huge crayfish eyed me, seeming to say: 'What have you come here for? Who are you?' Age-old eels. . . . – Often I was obliged to climb, swinging from branch to branch.

Reaching a détour——

what I saw – Description of the picture of *Pape Moë*——

Pl. 14; 47

I had made no sound. When she had finished drinking she took water in her hands and poured it over her breasts, then, as an uneasy antelope instinctively senses a stranger, she gazed hard at the thicket where I was hidden. Violently she dived, crying out the word *'tachae'* (fierce). . . . I rushed to look down into the water – vanished – Only a huge eel writhed between the small stones of the bottom. . . .

48   Arrival near Arorai – Legend of Tefatou.

For some time I had been depressed, my work was suffering – I was short of 49 50   many documents. It is true I had been divorced for some months. I was no longer forced to hear that babble, a *vahine* always asking me questions about the same things, and myself answering invariably with the same refrain – I decided to go off for a time on a journey round the island.

51   As I made up a few small parcels of what I would need on my way and tidied up all my sketches, my neighbour, friend Anani, watched me uneasily. At last he plucked up courage to ask me if I wanted to leave. I answered no, I was merely going to wander about for a while, I would come back. He did not believe me and wept. His wife came and joined him, and told me that she loved me, that I had no need of money to live there, that I could one day find rest there, – and she showed me, in her plot of ground near her hut, a place adorned by a shrub – I felt a longing to rest there for ever, sure that in eternity no one would come and disturb me. 'You Europeans always promise to stay, and when at last people love you you go away – to come back, you say, but you never come back——'

I dared not lie——

but at length [I said] 'I'll come back in a few days, I promise. Later I'll see.'

At length I set off.

VI

Journey round the island – Leaving the coast road I plunge into a thicket that leads far into the mountains. Arrive at a small valley. Several people live there and want to go on living in the old way——

Description of the picture *Matamua Autrefois* and of *Hina maruru*.

I move on. Arrived at Taravao (far end of the island) the gendarme lends me his horse, I ride along the East coast, not much frequented by Europeans. Arrived at Faone, the small district that comes before that of Itia, a native hails me. 'Hey! man who makes men' (he knows that I am a painter), 'come and eat with us *(Haere mai ta maha)*' – the phrase of welcome. I do not need to be asked twice, his face is so gentle. I dismount from the horse, he takes it and ties it to a branch, without any servility, simply and efficiently. I go into a house where several men, women and children are gathered, sitting on the ground chatting and smoking – 'Where are you going?' says a fine Maori woman of about forty. 'I'm going to Itia.' 'What for?' An idea passed through my brain. I answered: 'To look for a wife. Itia has plenty, and pretty ones.' 'Do you want one?' 'Yes.' 'If you like I'll give you one. She's my daughter.'

'Is she young?' 'AE'——

'Is she pretty?' 'AE'——

'Is she in good health?' 'AE'——

'Good, go and fetch her for me.'

She went away for a quarter of an hour; and as they brought the Maori meal of wild bananas and some crayfish, the old woman returned, followed by a tall young girl carrying a small parcel. Through her excessively transparent dress of pink muslin the golden skin of her shoulders and arms could be seen. Two nipples thrust out firmly from her chest. Her charming face appeared to me different from the others I had seen on the island up to the present, and her bushy hair was slightly crinkled. In the sunshine an orgy of chrome yellows. I found out that she was of Tongan origin.

When she had sat down beside me I asked her some questions:

'You aren't afraid of me?' '*Aita* (no).'

'Would you like to live always in my hut?' '*Eha.*'

'You've never been ill?' '*Aita.*'

That was all. And my heart throbbed as, impassively, she laid out on the ground before me, on a large banana-leaf, the food that was offered me. Though hungry, I ate timidly. That girl – a child of about 13 – enchanted me and scared me: what was going on in her soul? and at this contract so hastily thought of and signed I felt a shy hesitation about the signing – I, nearly an old man. Perhaps the mother had ordered it, with her mind on money. And yet in that tall child the independent pride of all that race . . . the serenity of a thing deserving praise. The mocking, though tender, lip showed clearly that the danger was for me, not for her. I left the hut, I will not say without fear, took my horse and mounted. The girl followed behind; the mother, a man and two young women – her aunts,

52

53; Pls. 72, 91

54

23 Studies. *c*.1891/3. Pencil and watercolour, 16.5 × 11 cm. Carnet de Tahiti, p. 12

she said – followed also. We took the road back to Taravao, 9 kilometres from
Faone – After a kilometre I was told: '*Parahi teie* (Stop here).' I dismounted and
entered a large hut, well kept and smelling almost opulent. The opulence of the
wealth of the earth. Pretty mats on the ground, on top of straw. . . . A family,
quite young and as gracious as could be, lived there, and the girl sat down next
to her mother, whom she introduced to me. A silence. Cool water, which we
drank in turn like a libation. And the young mother said to me, with tears in her
eyes: 'Are you kind?' . . .

When I had examined my conscience I answered uneasily: 'Yes.'

'Will you make my daughter happy?' 'Yes.'

'In 8 days let her come back. If she is not happy she will leave you.'

A long silence – We emerged and again I moved off on horseback. They followed behind. On the road we met several people. 'Well, well, you're the *vahine* of a Frenchman now, are you? Be happy. Good luck.'

That matter of two mothers worried me. I asked the old woman who had offered me her daughter: 'Why did you tell me a lie?' Tehamana's mother (that was my wife's name) answered: 'The other is also her mother, her nursing mother.'   55

We reached Taravao. I gave the gendarme back his horse.

His wife (a Frenchwoman) said to me (not indeed maliciously, but tactlessly): 'What! have you brought back a trollop with you?' And her eyes undressed the impassive girl, now grown haughty: decrepitude was staring at the new flowering, the virtue of the law was breathing impurely upon the native but pure unashamedness of trust, faith. And against that so blue sky I saw with grief this dirty cloud of smoke. I felt ashamed of my race, and my eyes turned away from that mud – quickly I forgot it – to gaze upon this gold which already I loved – I remember that. The family farewells took place at Taravao, at the house of the Chinese who there deals in everything – men and beasts. My fiancée and I took the public carriage, which brought us to Mataiea, 25 kilometres from there, – my home.

VII

My new wife was not very talkative, [she was] melancholy and ironic. We observed each other: she was impenetrable, I was quickly beaten in that struggle – in spite of all my inward resolutions my nerves rapidly got the upper hand and I was soon, for her, an open book——

Maori character (yields itself only in time)   56
French character

A week went by, during which I was childish to a point that surprised me. I loved her and I told her so, which made her smile. (She knew it perfectly well!) She seemed to love me and never told me so. Sometimes, at night, *flashes of light . . . played across Tehamana's golden skin.* That was all. It was a great   57
deal. That week, swift as a day, as an hour, was over: she asked me to let her go and see her mother at Faone. I had promised——

She left and sadly I put her in the public carriage with a few piastres in her handkerchief to pay the fare and give her father some rum. . . . To me it seemed a good-bye. Would she come back?

Several days later she came back.

I set to work again and happiness succeeded to happiness. Every day at the first ray of sun the light was radiant in my room. The gold of Tehamana's face flooded all about it, and the two of us would go naturally, simply, as in Paradise, to refresh ourselves in a near-by stream.

The life of every day – Tehamana yields herself daily more and more, docile and loving; the Tahitian *noa noa* pervades the whole of me; I am no longer conscious of the days and the hours, of Evil and of Good – all is beautiful – all is well. Instinctively, when I am working, when I am meditating, Tehamana keeps silence, she always knows when to speak to me without disturbing me. 58

Conversations about what happens in Europe, about God, about the Gods. She learns from me, I learn from her. . . .

In bed, at nightfall, conversations.

The stars interest her greatly: she asks me what the morning star and the evening star are called in French. She finds it hard to understand that the earth goes round the sun. She, in turn, tells me the names of the stars in her language. 59

Roua (great is his origin) slept with his wife, the dark earth; she gave birth first to her king the soil, then to the twilight, then to the dusk; but then Roua disowned this wife.

Roua (great is his origin) slept with the woman called 'great meeting'. She gave birth to the queens of the Heavens, the Stars, then to the Star *Faïti*, the evening star. The King of the gold Heavens, the only king, slept with his wife Fanoui. Of her was born Tauroua (Venus) the morning star, King Tauroua who 60 gives laws to the night and to the day, to the stars, to the Moon [and] to the Sun, and serves as guide to mariners. He set sail leftwards, towards the North; and there, sleeping with his wife, he begot the Red Star, that red star which shines at evening, under two aspects. . . . Red Star, that God, who flies in the west, made ready his pirogue, the pirogue of broad day, which scuds towards the skies. . . . He set sail at the rising of the sun, Rehoua. Rehoua advances in space. He slept with his wife *Oura Tanaipa*; of them were born the Kings, the twin ones facing the Pleiades. They were of Bora Bora. Having heard their parents talk of separating them, they left their father's house [and] went together to Raiatea, then to Outamé, to Eimeo and to Otaïti. Their mother, anxious, set out in search of them as soon as they had gone; but she always arrived at the various isles too late. However, at Otaïti she heard that they were still there and were hiding in the mountains; at length she found them, but they fled before her as far as the summit of the highest mountain; and there, just as, all in tears, she thought she had caught them at last, they flew off into the skies, where they can still be seen among the constellations.

What she would never admit is that those shooting stars, frequent in that country, crossing the sky slowly, in melancholy fashion, might be Tupapaüs.

One day I had to go to Papeete. I had promised to come back that same

24 *Hina. c.*1891/3. Tamanu wood and painted gilt, 37 × 13.4 × 10.8 cm. Gray 95. Hirshhorn Museum and Sculpture Garden, Smithsonian Institution, Washington

evening. On the way back the carriage broke down half way: I had to do the rest on foot. It was one in the morning when I got home. Having at that moment very little oil in the house – my stock was due to be replenished – the lamp had gone out, and the room was in darkness when I went in. I felt afraid and, more still, mistrustful. Surely the bird has flown. I struck matches and saw on the bed

Pl. 16; 61

(Description of the picture *Tupapau*)

The poor child came to herself again and I did all I could to restore her confidence. 'Never leave me alone again like this without light! What have you been doing in town? – you've been to see women, the kind who go to the market to drink and dance, then give themselves to the officers, to the sailors, to everybody?'

62

VIII

I was invited to a wedding, a real legal wedding – [a thing] which the missionaries have tried to impose on Christian converts. On the appointed day——

Under an improvised roof quickly run up by whoever was there and gracefully decorated with flowers and leaves, a large table. Relatives and friends are present and the food that day is sumptuous. Young pigs roasted whole over hot stones, a large quantity of fish, bread-fruits, wild bananas, taro, etc. . . . The local schoolmistress (a girl who was almost white) was marrying a real husband, a real Maori, the son of the chieftain of Punaauia. The girl had been at the church schools at Papeete, and the Protestant bishop, who was taking an interest in her, had insisted – urgently – on her marriage to the young chieftain. In those parts missionary's will is will of God. When everyone has eaten and drunk a great deal for an hour or so, the many speeches are delivered with order and method; eloquence and [the element of] surprise. – Which of the two families is to give the bride a new name is an important question, – often indeed the argument becomes almost a fight. There was nothing of the kind that day; all was calm, everyone [was] happy, gay and pretty drunk. My poor *vahine*, led on by some of the other girls (I was not keeping an eye on her), emerged dead drunk, and I had trouble in getting her home – very charming but very heavy. – In the place of honour at the table [sat] the admirably dignified wife of the chieftain of Punaauia, clad in an orange velvet dress: a pretentious, strange costume, very like those you see at a fair. And yet the inborn grace of that people [and] her consciousness of her rank made all that fancy dress beautiful; in the midst of all those flowers and Tahitian dishes, her fragrance was one more *noa noa*. Next to her sat a centenarian relative, a death-mask made yet more terrible by the intact double row of her cannibal teeth. Tattooed on her cheek, an indistinct dark mark, a shape like a letter. I had already seen tattoo-marks, but not like that one, which was certainly European. I was told that formerly the

63

missionaries had raged against indulgence and had branded some of the women on the cheek as a warning against hell, – a thing which covered them with shame (not shame for any sin committed, but the ridicule of a distinctive mark). When I heard that, I understood the present-day Maori's mistrust of Europeans.

Years have gone by between the old woman being marked by the priest and the girl being married by the priest. The mark is still there.

Five months later the bride gave birth to a well-formed child. . . . Fury of the relatives, who demanded a separation. The young man would have none of it: 'Since we love each other, what does it matter? It's one of our customs to adopt other people's children. I adopt this one.' – But why did the Bishop take such trouble to hurry on the legal marriage? . . .   64

Evil tongues insinuated that . . .

We prefer to believe in the angel of the annunciation.

IX

Tunny fishing – For about a fortnight the flies, rare till then, had been appearing   65 in swarms and becoming unbearable. And all the Maoris rejoiced, [for] the bonitos and tunny-fish would come in from the open sea. And set to work checking the strength of their lines and hooks. Women and children all lent a hand at dragging nets – or rather, long fences of coconut leaves – along the shore and over the coral rocks that form the bottom of the water between the land and the reefs. This to catch a small fish of which the tunnies are fond.

The day came when two large pirogues were launched in the sea, coupled together and bearing at the prow a very long rod that could be swiftly raised by two ropes stretching to the stern. By this means, when the fish has bitten, it is at once raised and brought aboard.

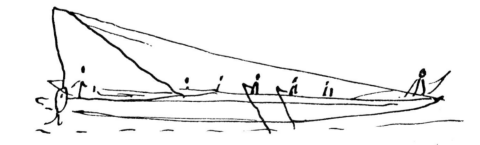

25 Fishing boat. *c.*1893. Pen and ink, 3 × 12 cm. Draft MS, p. 24

We pass between the reefs and move well out into the open sea. A turtle gazed at us going by.

We reach a place where the sea is very deep, known as the Tunny Hole: it is where they come to sleep at night, very deep down, out of reach of the sharks.

A cloud of sea-birds watch the tunny; when these come right to the surface, they drop to sea-level and rise again with a strip of flesh in their beak. Carnage on all sides——

When I asked why a long line was not let down into the Tunny Hole, I was told that it was a sacred place, the abode of the God of the Sea——

66   Legend – of Rouahatou——

This God, a sort of Neptune, was sleeping in the depths of the sea at that spot.

A fisherman committed the imprudence of going fishing there and, his hook having caught in the God's hair, the God was awakened. Furious, he came up to the surface to see who had been so bold as to disturb his sleep in this way; and when he saw that the culprit was a man, he at once decided that the whole human race should pay for this insult. The culprit alone was spared.

The God told him to go with all his family on to the *Toa Marama*, which some say is a pirogue, others an island or a mountain, but which I will call the Ark. Merely remarking that *Toa Marama* means 'Warrior of the Moon', which leads me to believe that the Ark (of whatever sort), and indeed the whole cataclysm, has some connection with the moon.

When the fisherman and his family had made their way to the appointed place, the waters of the sea began to rise and, quickly reaching the highest mountains, destroyed all beings except those that were on or in the *Toa Marama* and, later, re-peopled the islands or the earth.

A man was chosen by the captain of the boat to cast the hook clear of the pirogue. Time passed: not a tunny would bite. Another man was called. This time a superb fish bit – it made the rod bend. Four sturdy arms raised the stem and, with the tugging of the ropes from astern, the tunny was just being brought to the surface. A shark pounced on his prey. A few slashes of its teeth, and all we got into the boat was a head. The fishing was starting badly.

My turn came; I was chosen. A few moments, and we caught a huge tunny: a few blows on the head from a stick, and the animal, quivering in the death-throes, lay twisting its body, now transformed into glinting spangles of innumerable sparks. A second time we were fortunate: decidedly the French-man brought luck. They all shouted joyously that I was a fine fellow, and I, full of pride, did not say no. We fished till evening. When the supply of the small fish used as bait was exhausted, the sun was setting the horizon ablaze with red. We made ready to return. Ten magnificent tunnies overloaded the pirogues. While all was being put straight, I asked a young boy why [there had been] all those laughs and whispers at the moment when my two tunnies were brought aboard the pirogue. He refused to explain, but I insisted, knowing how little power of resistance a Maori has, how weak he is when pressed energetically. He then told me that a fish caught by the lower jaw means infidelity by your *vahine* while you are away fishing. I smiled incredulously. And we returned.

Night in the tropics advances swiftly. Twenty-two vigorous arms plunged the paddles into the sea, shouting excitedly in time. The powdery wake phos-phoresced, and it felt to me like some mad race, pursued by the mysterious spirits of the ocean and by the schools of curious fish that kept us company, leaping.

After two hours we were drawing near the entrance to the reefs, where the sea breaks violently. Dangerous place to pass because of the bar. To do so it is essential to keep the pirogue's bows well into the waves, but the natives are skilful and, not without a feeling of fear, I followed the manœuvre, which was carried out very well.

Before us, the shore, lit by moving fires (huge torches made out of dry coconut branches). The sea, the ground lit by those fires, and the families waiting, some seated motionless, others with the children running, jumping and uttering shrill cries. A powerful spirt of the pirogue, and it was high on the sand.

All our booty laid out on the sand. The captain cuts as many pieces – equal shares – as there were people engaged in the fishing – women and children as well – whether the main fishing or the fishing for the small fish. Thirty-seven shares.

Immediately afterwards my *vahine* took the axe, chopped wood [and] lit a fire, while I washed and put on some clothes against the coolness of the night.

My share of the fish cooked.

Hers raw.——

Countless questions. The incidents of the fishing. Bedtime came. One question was gnawing at me. What was the good? At last I asked it.

'Have you been good?' 'AE.'

'And was your lover today nice?' 'I have no lover.'

'You're lying. The fish has spoken.'

Her face took on a look I had never seen before, her brow expressed a prayer. In spite of myself I went with her in her faith – there are moments when warnings from on high are . . . useful.

Contrast between the religious – superstitious – faith of that race and the scepticism of our civilization.

Gently she closed the door and prayed aloud:

'Save me! Save me! It is evening; it is the evening of the Gods. Watch close by me, O my God! close by me, O my Lord. Keep me from the enchantments of evil conduct. From wishing evil or from cursing, from secret plotting. And from disputes over the boundaries of land; may peace reign about us.

'O my God, keep me against the furious warrior, from him who wanders in fury, takes pleasure in causing fear, – whose hair for ever bristles. Let me and my spirit live.

'O my God——'

That evening I prayed, almost.

Her prayer done, she drew near me, resigned, and said, with tears in her eyes: 'You must beat me, strike me hard.'

And before that resigned face, that marvellous body, I was reminded of some perfect idol. May my hands be forever accursed if they scourged a masterpiece

67

68 of creation! Naked like that, she seemed clothed in the orange-yellow garment of purity, the yellow mantle of Bhixu. A beautiful golden flower, whose Tahitian *noa noa* filled all with fragrance, and which I worshipped as an artist, as a man.

'Beat me, I tell you, or you'll be angry for a long time and you'll be ill.' I kissed her, and my eyes spoke these words of Buddha: 'It is by gentleness that anger must be conquered; by good that evil must be conquered; by truth lying.' That was a tropical night. Morning came radiant.

Mother-in-law brought us some fresh coconuts.

69 She questioned Tehamana with a look. She knew. Subtly she said to me: 'You went fishing yesterday. Did all go well?' I answered: 'I hope to go again very soon.'

X

70 I had to go back to France — imperative family duties called me back. — Goodbye, hospitable soil. — I went away two years older, younger by twenty years; more of a barbarian, too, and yet knowing more.

When I left the jetty to go aboard, Tehamana, who had wept for several nights [and was now] tired [and] melancholy, had sat down on the stone; her legs dangled, letting both her big sturdy feet brush the salt water. The flower she had been wearing over her ear had fallen into her lap, faded.

Others too, at various points, were watching, as though dazed, the heavy smoke of the ship that was carrying us all away, lovers of a day. And on the ship's bridge, using a spyglass, we could see upon their lips this old Maori

71 saying:

'You light breezes from the South and East, who join together to play and to caress one another above my head! make haste and run, all together, to the other island; you will see the man who has left me, as he sits in the shade of his favourite tree. Tell him you have seen me in tears.'

APPENDIX

After the work of art – The truth, the dirty truth.

Left France on an official mission. What made them give it to me? Perhaps some warning in the proper quarter, some warning from the crowd that examines, ransacks artists and later lays down the law. Perhaps to get rid of me with that pretence of a reward and never see me again. When taking leave of me: 'Don't be afraid to write to us so that we can repatriate you, as we did in the case of Monsieur D . . ., who was sent out to Japan. And when you come back we'll buy one or two of your works. As we did in the case of Monsieur D. . . . Our funds are distributed only *indirectly*. . . .'

What made me accept? . . . I don't know. . . . Poor, but rich in my art, I found I had to fall back on warships to get to Tahiti [and] to travel to the neighbouring islands where I planned to study.

On my arrival at Papeete my duty (since I was on an official mission) was to go and call on the Governor, the negro Lacascade, famous for his colour, for his *disreputable conduct*, for his earlier exploits at the Bank of Guadeloupe and, recently, for his exploits in the Leeward Islands. Despite all the complaints of King Pomaré and the cries of protest from the French colony, this sinister and incapable man was immovable. Throughout the ministry the reply was invariable *(debts to be paid back)*. Now only the person who had a wife or a daughter to offer him obtained a job from the sovereign distributor.

What corruption on all sides!

So it was sadly, and perhaps with the arrogance of disgust on my face, that I paid my call on the Governor, the negro Lacascade.

I was received with courtesy, indeed, the Ministry of Colonies having informed him that I was a painter, [and] with suspicion, for this profession, rare in Tahiti, was not very probable [and] that of political spy a more likely supposition. I withdrew, [and] that was all. And everyone was free to believe me other than I was. And yet I had long hair, no white helmet and, above all, no black suit. It was no use my declaring that I had no subsidies from the Government, that I was poor, simply an Artist – everyone kept on his guard. For in a town like Papeete there are many factions – Governor, Mayor, Protestant Bishop, Catholic missionaries, and the Ladies.

So much so that one holiday – July 14th – two magistrates' wives began tearing each other's hair in the public square, each accusing the other of the Governor's favour, and the husbands, respectable colonial magistrates, took each his wife's side and came to blows with their canes. The end, as usual, was a rebuff to the colony, and the two gentlemen received promotion.

It will be easily understood how anxious I was to escape from the town of Papeete, its officials and its soldiers – to get away and study and to prove at last that in that world I was *nothing*, a free man, an artist. In the end the obvious was accepted, and there were no more greetings.

After 18 months one of the magistrates – a decent man he was (probably in bad odour for that) – became concerned about the difficulties I had in working, and advised me to ask the Governor for the position of *juge de paix* in the Marquesas Islands. It had long been vacant, he said, and the job must be filled. It had previously been occupied by a high-grade official who was an incompetent fool, and in spite of the general council's repeated refusals the Governor had placed a favourite of his there, then repatriated him to France as an official with all the lavishness one could wish – this with no justification and by means of funds raised somehow or other and accounted for under Heading X. . . . It was almost a sinecure as regards the time it would take up, and so I would be able to go on with *useful work*.

This was really tempting the Devil. And yet I practically refused, asking for several days to think it over.

A week later, I had to go to Papeete.

The magistrate told me: 'You must strike the iron while it is hot. The *Procureur de la République* saw the Governor the other day; he mentioned your business and the Governor replied that he would be delighted to be of service to you.'

I crossed the square immediately (the conversation took place in front of Lacascade's palace) and, ashamed at asking anything of a despicable man (why is one dependent on despicable people?) and one who is despised, walked into the residence. The commissionaire sent my card up to the Governor and, five minutes later, asked me to go upstairs – the Governor was prepared to see me. And indeed there, at the head of the stairs, was Lacascade, in a black frock-coat and covered with scent as usual.

'Hullo, it's you, Monsieur Gauguin . . . I wasn't expecting to see you. And what brings you?'

'Simply a request I have to make to you, *Monsieur le Gouverneur*. As you know, I'm an artist. My researches in Tahiti are finished and I would like to go to the Marquesas Islands to continue them. I've just been *advised* to ask you for the position of *juge de paix*, which has long been vacant.'

'Ah, Monsieur Gauguin, what a wild idea you have had. And who, I wonder, can have suggested it to you? You don't know what *special aptitudes* are required in order to fill that delicate position, and what preliminary studies, etc. . . . No; honestly, it's impossible: it would be an appointment that would make the worst possible impression.' I marvelled at the genius of this humbug who, in a moment, at the first glance, could pronounce on my incompetence and informed me with such courtesy of the bad impression I would make as *juge de paix*.

I bowed and withdrew, like the fox, swearing that . . .

Later, when I had to go home, I wrote, trusting in the promises made to me at my departure, to the Beaux Arts, [explaining] my sad situation for getting home – journey expensive.

74 Five months later I had a two-fold answer:

26 Horned head. Photograph of a lost sculpture. Gray A-13. Louvre MS, p. 56

from the Beaux Arts request was made to 'dear Colleague' Monsieur Etienne of the [Ministry for] Colonies to do everything possible to bring home Monsieur Gauguin, an Interesting Artist who had been sent out on an official mission;

from the Secretary, same request to Tahiti: '*Monsieur le Gouverneur*, we would be grateful if you would *examine* if it is possible to arrange for the return home of . . .' Attached, the letter from the Beaux Arts.

The Governor did his duty – examined Conscientiously if it was possible. Absolutely impossible. Despite all our care in the administration of the funds Entrusted to us, the till is empty. . . .

There I was in Tahiti for another six months. . . .

As the result of countless complicated contracts and interventions by friends, the Minister of the Interior signed a repatriation order [for me] as a pauper, lowest grade – a thing which, abroad, every consul grants to Frenchmen adrift without means, and this on a mere request with immediate reply. What a treasure, what celerity, our Government departments!!

What was ordered was done; the Governor requested Commandant Manseron, captain of the *Duchaffault*, to offer me hospitality on board his ship, in the fo'c'sle, in the second-class petty-officers' quarters.

At the Tahiti office of the Ministry of the Interior I did all I could to have the request made for me to be in the ward-room; wasted effort – the order was explicit, signed and minuted. Luckily the *Duchaffault* was not a ship stationed locally and its captain was not under orders from M. Lacascade: luckily the officers with some idea of things in France had heard of me as an Artist, recognized in me a decent person and agreeable company, and invited me to join them in the ward-room. As I came aboard, the captain, a gentleman as they usually are in the Navy, said to me: 'Monsieur Gauguin, you are welcome.' I travelled in this way as far as Noumea: these gentlemen did everything possible to make life for me pleasant. Their names were:

Monsieur Allemand (second-in-command)
    „   Faure
    „   Martin
    „   Clergeau
    „   Mazet
    „   Godet

I am happy to be able to pay tribute to them here and to express my whole-hearted gratitude.

At Noumea, forced to wait twenty days for the liner, and that at my own cost (as a *pauper*, such was my repatriation): it was hard. I left at last on the Messageries liner, so luxuriously fitted up for first and second classes. I left, huddled forward in the third class, penned in with 200 private soldiers, having fifty square centimetres per man in which to move about on the deck forward, in the midst of chained-up sheep and cattle. Forty days like that. God, it's long. If it weren't for the sea, one would rather walk home.

75

I am here at last, among my own people and my friends. And while I have to complain of the silence on the part of the heads of the Beaux Arts [and] of the *failure to keep all the promises made to me when I was sent out*, I have received from artists, thinkers, etc., the one recompense for my intellectual efforts.

On board, I found myself once more in the company of the negro Lacascade, who was on his way to Mayotte where he has been appointed – probably to run up fresh debts there and replenish his harem.

When I say I was in his company once more, that is a bad way of expressing myself: I heard he was on board; barriers indicate to the passengers the limits of where they may go. A special saloon is reserved for our lords and masters, whose excursions must not be too arduous.   76

Three more stories from Noa Noa

There are three episodes among the narrative chapters of the Louvre MS that do not appear in the Draft MS, but which were certainly drafted by Gauguin at around the same time. Each of the three stories is convincing as having a basis in Gauguin's life in Tahiti and it is inconceivable that they were originated by Morice, whose role in relation to Gauguin's material for *Noa Noa* was always that of responsive elaborator, never of inventor. In the case of one story – that of Princess Vaïtua – we know of the existence of a Gauguin manuscript: Morice published the first page of it in the 1920 edition of his monograph (Plate 62). It is only reasonable to assume lost manuscripts for the others.

The only doubts, provoked as with a forged painting by detailed correspondence to a single authenticated work, arise from the similarities between the Grotto of Mara story and that of the young woodcutter in Chapter IV of the Draft MS. In both we find the warning *'Toe Toe'*, descriptions of echoes ringing against the rocks, and the talk of Gauguin's conversion to a Maori state. Against such suspicions, we must set Gauguin's habit of repetition. For the rest, the Grotto anecdote is alive with fresh narrative detail, with asides that exhibit both Gauguin's characteristic bravado and his characteristic neuroses and, finally, with the cross-fertilization of fact and fantasy that is *Noa Noa*'s autograph hallmark.

The story of Princess Vaïtua

Ia Orana Gauguin.

It was the princess who entered my room. I was on my bed dressed only in a simple pareo. No way to receive a woman of class.

You are ill, she said to me. I have come to see you.

And what is your name I asked——

Vaïtua.

Vaïtua was a true princess if indeed any still exist, since the Europeans have reduced everything in this country to their own level. In fact, she arrived there with bare feet, a flower at her ear and wearing a black dress. She was in mourning for her uncle, the King Pomaré, who had just died.

Her father Tamatoa, despite his constant contact with European life through receptions at the admiral's house, had never wanted anything but the life of a royal Maori. He was a fearsome striker of men in moments of anger and a terrible minotaur at revelries. It was said that Vaïtua was very like him.

Like any European arriving innocently in the island, I looked at this fallen princess with a sceptical smile, but I wanted to be polite so I said——

It is very friendly of you to come here, would you like to drink an absinthe with me and I pointed to a bottle that I had recently bought for guests.

Coolly and without expression she went to the place indicated and stooped to pick up the bottle. Her light transparent gown stretched tight against her loins, loins fit to bear a world – there was no mistake – this was indeed a princess. Her ancestors? mighty and courageous giants.

Her head was planted firmly on her shoulders. For a fleeting moment I saw only the jaws of a cannibal, the teeth that tore flesh, and a passing expression on her face that was of a cunning animal; despite her very fine, noble forehead, she seemed wholly unattractive.

I hoped that she would not come to sit on my bed, since the feeble structure would never support the two of us. But this is just what she did, and despite loud creaking, the bed survived. We got to know each other while drinking. From time to time conversation lapsed and the silence embarrassed me. I looked at her. She was watching me. But the bottle was emptying. Vaïtua drank solidly. The sun was setting fast – Vaïtua rolled a Tahitian cigarette and then stretched out on the bed. Her naked feet caressed the wooden bedpost like the tongue of a

27 Overleaf left: *Hina Tefatou* (also called The Moon and the Earth). s. & d. 1893. 112 × 62 cm. W499. Museum of Modern Art, New York

28 Overleaf right: *Parau na te varua Ino* (Words of the Devil). s. & d. 1892. 94 × 70 cm. W458. National Gallery, Washington

tiger around a skull. Her strange expression was both softer and more animated. I could almost hear the purring of a cat as it contemplates some fearful act of sensuality – how one changes! because now I found her beautiful, very attractive. And when she said to me in a halting voice 'You are nice', I was deeply moved. I knew now, without any doubt at all, that the princess was delicious.

Then in a very serious coppery voice, she recited the whole of Lafontaine's fable, The Cricket and the Ant. A charming memory of her childhood among the nuns who educated her.

The cigarette was almost all burned; she stood up——

You know Gauguin, she said to me, I don't like your Lafontaine.

What! But we call him the *great* Lafontaine.

Perhaps he is great, but he bores me with his wretched morals.

The ants! (and her mouth turned up in disgust). The crickets!

How I love the crickets – it's so lovely to sing, so good.

To sing always

To give . . . always

And she added passionately, 'What a beautiful kingdom ours used to be, a place where both man and the earth abounded in natural riches. We used to sing throughout the year.

'I think I have drunk plenty of absinthe, I am leaving, I shall do something stupid.'

Vaïtua disappeared, calling *uri* (dog).

I put my head back on the pillow and in my ear heard (like a whisper) this phrase

Ia Orana Gauguin

Ia Orana Princess

I rested . . .

(Louvre MS, pp. 36–9)

The story of the Ear-rings

Tehura was sometimes very loving and very wise, sometimes silly and full of frivolity, two very different beings in one, which could succeed each other with the most disconcerting speed. It was not so much a question of her changing as of a dual personality – the child of an ancient race.

One day the ubiquitous itinerant Jew, who scours the earth, arrived in the district selling trinkets of gilded copper. He spread out his wares and everyone crowded round him. A pair of ear-rings was passed from hand to hand and all eyes lit up, all the women coveted them.

Tehura looked at me, her brow wrinkled. Her eyes made it clear that she wanted them. I pretended not to understand.

She drew me aside:

– I want them.

I explained that in France such a trifle would cost only two francs, that they were made from copper.

Noatou – I want them.

But it would be stupid to pay twenty francs for such rubbish! No.

– I want them.

And with a passionate urgency, her eyes full of tears: What? Wouldn't you be ashamed to see this jewel on the ears of another woman! Already someone else talks of selling his horse in order to offer the ear-rings to his *vahine*.

I would not give in to this stupidity and this time I refused vehemently.

Tehura looked at me once again, defeated; without a word she wept.

I went away, came back, gave the twenty francs to the Jew – and the sun shone again.

It was Sunday two days later. Tehura was dressing herself up. Her hair was washed with soap, then dried in the sun and finally rubbed with fragrant oil; with her dress, one of *my* handkerchiefs in her hand, a flower at her ear and bare feet, she was off to the temple, repeating the psalms that she would soon recite there.

And your ear-rings? I said to her.

Tehura pouted disdainfully:

They're just copper! *Aita Piro, Pirupiru.*

And with a shriek of laughter she walked out of the door and left for the temple – becoming serious again.

At siesta time, undressed, naked, we slept side by side, on this day as on any other, or we dreamt – maybe in her dream Tehura saw other ear-rings sparkling. As for me, I should rather forget all I know and sleep always . . .

(Louvre MS, pp. 110–12)

29 *Vairaoumati Tei Oa* (Her name is Vairaoumati). s. & d. 1892. 91 × 60cm. W450.
Hermitage, Leningrad

30 Tahitian figures. *c*.1896/7. Watercolour. Louvre MS, p. 173

The story of the Grotto of Mara

77 Heaven knows what time of year it was – because the sun always shines – when the two of us set out one morning to visit some friends whose house was 10 kilometres away. Leaving in the cool at 6 o'clock we made such good time that we arrived there by around half past eight. We were not expected and the rejoicing that greeted us was concluded with the hunt of a young pig. It was slaughtered – two chickens were added; and with a superb octopus caught that

78 morning, several *taros* and bananas, our feast became sumptuous and succulent.

I proposed that we should pass the rest of the morning by going to the grotto of Mara which I had often skirted on my travels but never thought of visiting.

A young boy, three young girls and Tehura and I made up the happy bunch who set off for the jaunt: the grotto was close by. Hidden almost entirely by guava trees, the grotto looked from the road no more than a cleft in the rocks. But if you pulled back the branches and slithered a metre or so down the bank, you were in a dark cavity. Away from the brilliant sunlight above, your eyes could see nothing; then they perceived a grotto whose further end, about a 100 metres away, looked like a small theatre set, with no curtains but with a bright red ceiling. Against the walls on each side what looked like enormous serpents were gliding slowly, as if coming to drink at the surface of this underground lake. They are roots which have made their life among the crevices in the rocks.

I proposed a swim, but in vain: they said that the water was very cold. Lengthy secret discussions followed and then giggles, which made me curious. I insisted. At last the girls agreed and stripping off light clothes, we were all in the water.

79 Only the general cry of *toe toe* could be heard: the water rippled all around and then the echo *Toe toe* came back.

– 'Are you coming with me?' I asked Tehura pointing to the far end.

'Are you mad? It's very far over there . . . and the eels! No one ever goes there.'

And undulating gracefully at the water's edge, she played in the water with an adolescent pride in her swimming. But I was no less proud of my own skill as a swimmer and I set off, my heart beating at the prospect of going alone. I experienced the strange illusion that the far end of the cave was receding, the more I swam towards it. I went on forwards and on each side the serpents watched ironically. At one moment I thought I saw a huge tortoise floating by and then, more clearly still, its head rise up out of the water to confront me. What absurd thoughts! – sea turtles don't live in fresh water. Was I mad or had I become a true Maori, subject to their myths and superstitions. At that moment my doubts were too strong, and I was almost afraid, filled with apprehension. And those undulations ahead of me – the eels!

I had to overcome this terror and I dived suddenly down to touch the bottom; I didn't reach it and I re-surfaced. I had not even touched the bottom to regain my confidence.

Tehura called me: Come back——

I turned back and saw her, far away: how was it that the distances there always seemed to reach to infinity: Tehura was no more than a black speck in a pool of light.

I was determined to have the last word and I swam furiously for about half an hour. Eventually after an hour, I touched the edge.

A small ordinary plateau beside a yawning hole – which went where? Mystery. I have to admit that I was frightened.

I came back . . . only Tehura was waiting: her friends had lost interest and left.

Tehura said a prayer and we started back.

In the open air, the trembling from my ordeal subsided, I became warm again and I felt alive.

I think there was irony in Tehura's smile as she asked me: Weren't you afraid?

Shamelessly, I replied: We French, we are never afraid.

There was no sign of admiration from Tehura. And she found it quite natural that a little further on I should pick some fragrant flowers for her hair. The road was beautiful, the sea superb, Morea in front of us, grandiose and arrogant: it was good to be alive and to devour the pig that awaited our arrival.

80

(Louvre MS, pp. 138–42)

31 Top: *Te Po* (The night) (fragment). *c*.1894/5. Woodcut. From an unnumbered page of the Louvre MS (see Guérin 15)

32 *Auti te Pape* (Women by the river). *c*.1894/5. Woodcut, 20.5 × 35.5. Guérin 35. Museum of Modern Art, New York

33 Opposite: *Nave Nave Fenua* (Delicious land). *c*.1894/5. Colour woodcut, 34.5 × 20 cm. Guérin 29. Museum of Modern Art, New York

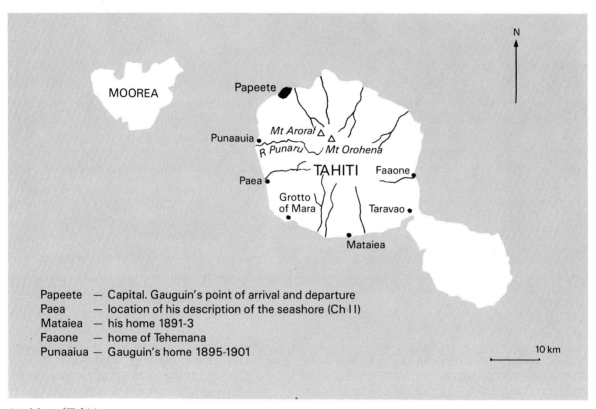

34 Map of Tahiti

Noa Noa   Notes to Gauguin's manuscript

1   A whole section – nineteen lines of manuscript – is crossed through at the start of Gauguin's draft. They read as follows:

> I do not know why the government granted me this mission – probably to give the impression of having sponsored an artist. One does know however, how much it would cost a director of the Beaux Arts to let it happen. I don't know why I made this journey with this piece of paper in my pocket? It is that to arrive there one has sometimes to travel by a government boat and one can very easily end up in the sailors' quarters. Thanks to my document, courtesy of M. Guarou, Director of the Interior at Noumea, I embarked on the *Vire*, in the officers' ward room. It wasn't the same coming back——

> The negro Lacascade, governor of Tahiti, requested a passage for me from the master of the Duchuffault . . . Despite everything, one sometimes meets with courtesy, above all when one is at sea. Captain Manseron . . . and all the other officers . . . welcomed me openly and I was duly installed in the officers' quarters. Thanks to these gentlemen, I came back to France agreeably enough.

(See also Note 72)

35   Caricature of Governor Lacascade. *c.*1892/3. Pen and wash

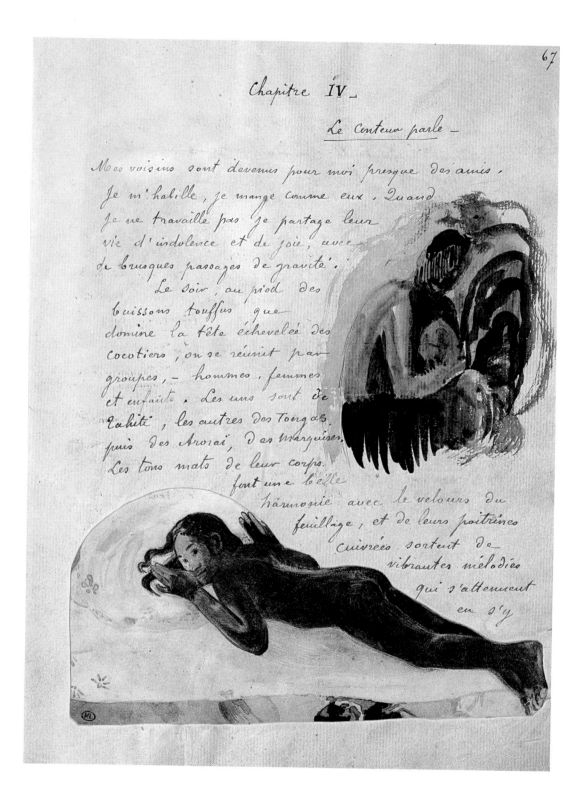

Chapitre IV_

Le Conteur parle _

Mes voisins sont devenus pour moi presque des amis.
Je m'habille, je mange comme eux. Quand
je ne travaille pas je partage leur
vie d'indolence et de joie, avec
de brusques passages de gravité.

Le soir, au pied des
buissons touffus que
domine la tête échevelée des
cocotiers, on se réunit par
groupes, — hommes, femmes
et enfants. Les uns sont de
Tahiti, les autres des Tongas,
puis des Aroraï, des Marquises.
Les tons mats de leur corps
font une belle
harmonie avec le velours du
feuillage, et de leurs poitrines
cuivrées sortent de
vibrantes mélodies
qui s'atténuent
en s'y

36 p. 67 of the Louvre MS

37 Photograph of Tahitiennes; watercolour of Hina and Tefatou. p. 55 of the Louvre MS

38 *Portrait of Suzanne Bambridge.* s. & d. 1891. 70 × 50 cm. W423. Musées Royaux, Brussels

2   There is some conflict between accounts of the date of Gauguin's first arrival in Tahiti. Lieutenant Jénot, who met Gauguin at the dock, mentions the surprise arrival of the ship *La Durance* from New Caledonia 'one morning in the month of June 1891' (Wildenstein 1958, p. 116).

Apart from Gauguin's mention of a 63-day journey ending on June 8th, he says in a letter, which Malingue dates June 4th, 1891, 'the post happens to be leaving today, three days after our arrival'; in another letter that the King had died 'a few days after our arrival'; and in a third that he arrived fifteen days before the death of the King (Malingue, *Letters,* 1948, pp. 161, 162 and 166). King Pomaré died on June 12th and was buried on June 16th.

Rotonchamp's 1906 biography had established that Gauguin left Paris for Marseilles on April 4th and this was not challenged until Perruchot (1961) and Danielsson (1966), both claiming the authority of maritime records, stated that he left Marseilles on April 1st, 1891 aboard the *Océanien*, changed at New Caledonia onto *La Vire* and docked in Tahiti on the morning of June 9th. This makes a total of seventy days inclusive. Gauguin's mention of *La Vire* in the passage quoted in Note 1 above would seem to confirm this, despite the conflict over ships' names with the normally dependable testimony of Jénot.

3   Moorea is a neighbouring island to the northwest of Tahiti, within the Society Islands group. Gauguin refers to it twice more in *Noa Noa,* at the start of Chapter II of the Draft MS and at the conclusion of the 'Grotto of Mara' story (see p. 57). In *Avant et Après,* Gauguin describes sitting on his balcony watching the sun set behind Moorea (p. 17). In the memoirs of the American painter John Lafarge, Moorea is mentioned as ever-present on the horizon; Lafarge writes of its 'fantastic peaks and crags' and of the island 'glowing like a rose at the beginning of twilight' (Lafarge 1914, p. 305). See also Danielsson 1966, p. 91.

4   The much-travelled one is of course Gauguin himself. He alludes here to his extensive travels in the French and Merchant Navies, 1865–71. As a 17-year-old apprentice he had made at least two trips to Rio de Janeiro on the *Luzitano* in 1865 and 1866.

Perruchot has reconstructed other journeys on the *Chili,* 1866–7, to South America and Polynesia, and in 1868, on the French Navy's *Jérome-Napoléon,* to the Mediterranean, the Black Sea, Naples, Venice and London (Perruchot 1961, pp. 54–7). In an article in *Les Guêpes,* June 12th, 1899, Gauguin recalled a train journey from Folkestone to London and visits to Madame Tussaud's and the London Zoo (Danielsson & O'Reilly 1966, p. 22).

5   Lacascade, a native of Guadeloupe, had been Governor of the French Oceanic Settlements for five years when Gauguin first arrived (Danielsson 1966, pp. 62–4). His initial respect for Gauguin steadily gave way to a mutual animosity. In Gauguin's caricature (Pl. 35), as Danielsson explains, there is both the visual pun of the profiles and a verbal pun on the double meaning of '*magot*' ('baboon' and 'treasure'). It was alleged locally that Lacascade had put together a small fortune, the fruits of corrupt administration. See also the bitter comments in the Appendix to *Noa Noa* (pp. 43–7).

6   There was nothing exceptional about the fact that Gauguin had been granted an official 'mission' to Tahiti. He secured it in 1891, with the support of Charles Morice and other friends in Paris, after successive applications to the Ministries of Education and the Colonies and the Director of the Beaux Arts. The 'mission' did not require anything of Gauguin. It afforded him assistance with his sea passage; the promise of purchase of a painting or paintings for 3,000 francs on his return and – potentially important – it guaranteed him the sort of respectful reception from authorities and the colonial community that Gauguin describes in his early letters from Papeete. The bearers of unspecified artistic missions were always treated with cautious respect and attention. Apparently the guise was sometimes used as a cover for government investigators, hence Gauguin's mention here of 'spying'.

Had Gauguin wished to capitalize on this circumstance, he could have sustained a flow of portrait commissions, as a source of income, from the European community (Malingue, *Letters,* 1948, p. 162). The portrait of Miss Bambridge is one of only a tiny handful that we know Gauguin made at the time. Miss Bambridge, an Englishwoman married to a Tahitian chief, belonged to the upper ranks of Papeete society. The portrait was not well received.

When in Panama in 1887, Gauguin wrote that while his companion, the painter Charles Laval, could earn money from portraits, he himself was incapable of painting them badly enough to be accepted! (Malingue, *Letters,* 1948, p. 80).
(See also Note 73)

7   Even though Pomaré V was indeed the last King of Tahiti, his death in 1891 was only nominally a sign

39 Left: King Pomaré V. Photograph from the Louvre MS, p. 37

40 Right: Queen Marau. Photograph

of 'taking-over' by the French, whose colonial authority was already comfortably and irrevocably established.

Lafarge describes Pomaré as 'a handsome elderly man, somewhat broken and far from sober' who had 'surrendered his rights to the French a few years ago, under long pressure and with some advice from the missionaries. In exchange he received an annual income and retained his honours and certain privileges' (Lafarge 1914, pp. 308–10).

(See also Notes 8, 13)

8 Pomaré V died on June 12th, 1891 and the funeral that Gauguin describes later in this chapter took place on June 16th.

Gauguin had an appointment to see Pomaré on the very morning of his death, and had been hoping for royal patronage. 'Tomorrow I am going to see all the Royal Family', he wrote to his wife. 'All of which is advertisement, however tiresome' (Malingue, *Letters*, 1948, p. 162).

9 Unlike King Pomaré, from whom she was separated soon after their marriage, Queen Marau (1860–1934) was devoted to the recording of Maori culture (see Lafarge 1914, p. 345; Danielsson 1966, p. 65).

A volume of her memoirs – which is principally a compilation by her of the memoirs of her mother Arii Taimai – was published privately in 1893 by Henry Adams, friend of Marau's brother Tati and travelling companion of John Lafarge. Adams wrote that when Marau disappeared, there would be no other person on the island with an exact knowledge of its past.

Like Gauguin, Adams was impressed by Marau's exceptional looks and bearing. He romanced that 'one can sense in her the 100 generations of chiefs from whom she is descended' (Salmon/Adams 1980, p. 12). R. L. Stevenson had been befriended by the same family during his visit to Tahiti in 1888.

Gauguin had no access to this circle. He did not speak English and anyway usually chose to associate with less elevated levels of society. The one main exception among his friends was the Chief Tetuanui, a long-standing adversary of Tati's family, who introduced Gauguin to what he could of Maori tradition. Tetuanui later told Frederick O'Brien of a visit to an ancient *marae* (open-air Maori temple or meeting place). Gauguin was very disappointed at its ruined state (*The Century Magazine*, June 1920. Quoted in Teilhet-Fisk 1983, p. 45).

10   In the margin of Gauguin's manuscript at this point there appears the letter 'A': a reference to the 'Diverse notes' jotted down on an earlier blank page. The relevant section of those notes reads as follows:

> The sculptural form of over there—
> Two columns of a temple, simple and erect—
> Two eyes of the breasts
> And the vast height culminating in a point
> the great triangle of the Trinity—
> the power of on high—

In the Louvre MS (p. 30), the following version of the note appears after the phrase 'a real impressiveness':

> She had that majestic sculptural quality so typical there, ample and at the same time gracious with arms like two columns of a temple, simple, erect, and the vast height culminating in a point – a bodily construction which evokes forever in my mind the great triangle of the *Trinity*.

The relationship between the fragmentary note and the text was already cryptic in Gauguin's own manuscript, but the awkward transitions in Morice's prose above suggest that he might not have really understood Gauguin's intention. However, we must also remember, as always, that the Louvre MS was copied out by Gauguin himself, implying his approval.

11   The phrase 'their breasts leading and the conical shells which tipped their nipples drawing the muslin of their dresses to a point' was added as an afterthought in the margin of the original manuscript.

12   The words *Noa Noa* here make their first appearance in the manuscript. Gauguin drafted the translation of *Teine Merahi Noa Noa* as 'now that smells good', but then struck it out in favour of 'now very fragrant'.

We do not know when or how the title of *Noa Noa* first emerged. It appears that no manuscript is referred to as *Noa Noa* in letters before 1895, when Morice wrote: 'I have a complete manuscript of our *Noa Noa*' (Loize 1966, p. 81). In an interview in May 1895, Gauguin gave the title as '*Noa Noa* – a Tahitian word meaning "fragrant"'.

Danielsson suggests that the noun '*Fenua*' is implied in the phrase *noa noa* and that we should

41 *Notes Diverses*. From a flyleaf of the Draft MS (see Note 10 above)

properly translate it as 'Fragrant Land' or 'The Fragrant Isle'. He is all the more convincing when he relates it to Moerenhout's description of the Tahitian paradise: 'They had a celestial abode called *Rohutu noanoa*.' The quotation comes from the very chapter in Moerenhout which Gauguin raided most heavily for the *Ancien Culte Mahorie* (Danielsson 1966, pp. 169–70; Moerenhout 1837, I, p. 434).

L. J. Bouge translates *Noa Noa*, the title of an 1892 painting (now lost, W487), as 'Fragrant nature' (Wildenstein 1958, p. 162).

13 This linking of vanishing customs with Pomaré's death is more of a literary device than anything else, since the King had done little to sustain Maori traditions. Danielsson (1966, p. 64) paints the true picture:

> the most surprising circumstance connected with the King was that he should have lived to be 52. The primary cause of the King's demise was his huge thirst, which he had inherited with a fortune big enough to quench it. To drink oneself to death, in fact, was a royal tradition.

The same traditions prevailed elsewhere in the Pacific. In 1889, R. L. Stevenson wrote home to Charles Baxter about King Kalaku of Hawaii: 'a very fine intelligent fellow, but oh, Charles, what a crop for the drink!' One of a line of royal alcoholics, he also died in 1891 (Johnstone 1905, pp. 52–3).

This drinking may be seen as just another face of the colonialist erosion of indigenous life. The alcohol was mostly imported and much of the excessive drinking was apparently undertaken for the entertainment of Europeans, settlers and visitors. Alcoholism and disease were two major European contributions to the decimation of the native population of Tahiti. Gauguin himself was not innocent in these respects. His *Maison du Jouir* in the Marquesas was popular with natives as a plentiful source of free rum and claret and Gauguin had arrived in Tahiti already suffering from syphilis. (See also Note 21)

42 Converted Raratongans surrendering their images of gods to missionaries. Engraving. *Missionary Enterprises*, London, 1837

14 The two rows of dotted lines are in Gauguin's original manuscript, suggesting either reference to another draft of this paragraph, or – more likely – the indication of an idea that is still to be finally thought out. In the Louvre MS (pp. 32–3), we find the resolution:

> I was seized by a profound sadness. To have travelled so far only to find the very thing from which I had fled! The dream which led me to Tahiti was cruelly contradicted by the present: It was the Tahiti of times past that I loved. And I could not resign myself to the belief that it was totally destroyed, that this beautiful race was no more, that nothing had survived of its ancient splendour. How should I manage to recover the traces of that past. . . .

It is typical of what the Louvre MS has to tell us about the collaboration over *Noa Noa* that this passage, so characteristic of Gauguin in its mood as well as in its blend of realism and artifice, appears to have been drafted by Charles Morice.

15 The two issues here, first the general lack of material available to him and secondly the enormous support that Gauguin received from one single source – Moerenhout's *Voyages aux Iles du Grand Océan* (1837) – are discussed later (pp. 108–19).
    Gauguin repeatedly laments the lack of any indigenous art and appears to have recognized very rapidly that the 'civilizing' effect upon Tahiti of European settlers and traders on the one hand, and of Protestant and Catholic missions from England and France on the other, had reduced the fire in the 'ancient hearth' to ashes some half a century earlier. (See Jénot (in Wildenstein 1958); Danielsson 1966; *Avant et Après*.)

16 In the publicity surrounding Gauguin's 1893 exhibition of Tahitian paintings in Paris, great play was made of the fact that, unlike Pierre Loti and other 'dabblers' in primitive culture, Gauguin did not stay long in the Europeanized capital, but made straight for the 'bush'. (See the cuttings from contemporary newspapers in Gauguin's *Cahier pour Aline*.)
    It appears that Gauguin had his first short spell in the country at Paea, 13 miles south of Papeete, probably in August 1891. His permanent departure from Papeete was delayed by hospital treatment for 'a haemorrhage'. Gauguin himself refers to several days' illness caused by bronchitis contracted the previous winter in Paris (Louvre MS, p. 36). Biographers now agree that he was undergoing treatment for the second stage of syphilis (Danielsson 1966, pp. 89–92).
    When Gauguin did leave, in September 1891, it was to the district overseen by Chief Tetuanui. Tetuanui was a Francophile; under the auspices of the government he had visited Paris in 1889 for the Exposition Universelle. He met Gauguin and befriended him in Papeete at the time of Pomaré's funeral. He lived in the south of the main island and was Gauguin's introduction to Mataiea. (See also Note 9.)
    Tahiti's larger island, Tahiti Nui, comprises a simple volcanic cone with Mt Orohena (7,339 ft; 2,237 m) at its centre. The precipitous interior is virtually uninhabitable. Gauguin travelled south and then east around the ribbon of coast to Mataiea – 'always to the right the sea'. Mataiea is about twenty-four miles (45 km) from Papeete. Gauguin was to live there until 1893 (see map p. 60).

17 There is no clue in Gauguin's original truncated phrase '*Puis je v.*' to suggest more than the possibility of '*Puis je voulais*' (wanted). In the Louvre MS (p. 34) it is left out altogether.

18 By a slip of the pen in the Draft MS, Gauguin wrote here: 'Titi asked me if I would agree to take her with *her*.'

19 In the margin of the manuscript, Gauguin wrote 'B' against this line. The reference is picked up by the note 'See B' a few pages later, where the narrative is describing his parting from Titi, because she was already too tainted by civilization. (See Note 36.)
    Maybe the note was to draw Morice's attention to the correspondence between the two passages when he came to rewrite? Neither passage is significantly different in the Louvre MS.

20 The literal meaning of *Mau Saisis* in the manuscript is not clear. In his text of the Draft MS (Loize 1966, p. 21), Loize alters the phrase to read '*mau = saisir*' (i.e. *mau* means to seize), which makes a lot more sense.

21 This almost certainly refers to venereal diseases which Europeans, Gauguin included, brought to Tahiti. Epidemic disease had been a major cause of massive reductions of the native population – maybe from as much as 70,000 (Cook's estimate around the time of the island's 'discovery' in the

1760s) to as little as 7,000 when the French formally took over the island some seventy years later (Bovis 1855, pp. 10–13). Other estimates suggest that the 1760s population may have been as high as 100,000 or even 150,000 (Danielsson 1966, pp. 88–9; Phelps 1976, p. 110), but, as Bovis points out, since habitable land was more or less restricted to the half-mile-wide coastal ribbon around the island, it is difficult to imagine where they all lived.

22 Andersen's writing about Gauguin, for all its racy style, has focused useful suspicion on some of the more extravagant autobiographical episodes. In this context, he casts doubt on Gauguin's account of his affair with Titi, whose notoriety was something of a legend among the European community. 'Was Titi simply inserted into his recurrent fantasy of the fateful woman, as a device to define his innocent Eve?' Andersen asks (*Writings of a Savage*, p. xiii). (But see also Andersen's earlier extensive analysis of the relationship with Titi in his *Gauguin's Paradise Lost*, 1971, pp. 163–5, 224.)
    Some support for Andersen's scepticism may be gleaned from reading Gauguin's description of his encounter with Princess Vaïtua (Three more stories, pp. 49–52), which in the Louvre MS is inserted into the narrative at this point on pp. 36ff.

23 The sequence of paragraphs in Gauguin's manuscript is debatable at the start of this chapter. Two additional small sheets of text, written on both sides, are pasted onto the margin of page 7 of his manuscript. At the top of that page are the notes that we begin with – 'Description landscape, etc. . . .' These are clearly notes for further development and the two stuck-in additions are part at least of that projected development, picking up the first ('shore side') and second ('picture of the woodcutter') cues. Jonathan Griffin's translation follows this sequence.
    Loize (1966, pp. 21ff) concludes differently, apparently on the basis of the Louvre MS (pp. 38ff).

24 From the description that follows, this shore was probably at Paea, where Gauguin stayed briefly with a schoolteacher friend in July/August 1891 (Danielsson 1966, pp. 90–1).

25 The drawing of a crested head (Plate 6) was added to the manuscript in explanation of this image. The first paragraph here is not easy to translate: Griffin's literal transcription preserves the raw material of Gauguin's image. His sharp eye for an evocative, allusive silhouette has been stimulated by the eccentric contour of the black cliffs against the sunset. His imagination takes over from there.

26 Other visitors to Tahiti were struck by the same phenomenon. Lafarge wrote of 'a silence so great that the slightest rustle of a sail or cordage, or steps on deck could be distinctly heard' (Lafarge 1914, pp. 342–3). (See also p. 146.)

27 This description relates closely to the painting *Man with an Axe* (Plate 5) and, in some respects, to *Matamoë* (Plate 80). One of these two paintings must have been the 'Woodcutter of Pia' listed in Gauguin's *Carnet de Tahiti*, pp. 2–3. (See Wildenstein 1964, pp. 168–9; Field 1977, p. 101.)

28 The linguistic connection of Atua with Taäta appears to be Gauguin's invention. The instinct to identify common sources for all religious faiths was very much in the air in Theosophist circles in Paris (Gauguin's friends Sérusier and Schuffenecker were both involved) and it became a recurrent theme in Gauguin's writing.
    In Tahiti it may well have been encouraged by the interpretative commentary in Moerenhout's book which, in its respectable way, ploughs a similar furrow, making frequent cross-cultural connections.

29 Inasmuch as *Noa Noa* is an account of Gauguin's actual life in Tahiti, the text from here on refers to his stay in Mataiea.
    In the margin of the manuscript alongside this first paragraph, down as far as 'Rightly perhaps', Gauguin added this thematic sub-heading: *'apprivoisement d'un côté et d'autre'* (each side gets used to the other).

30 Gauguin's answers vary to the recurrent question 'Why did I hesitate . . .?' Earlier in *Noa Noa* (p. 12), he explains 'I was in some ways blind' in similar terms: 'Having only just arrived, rather disappointed as I was . . .' etc.
    In a letter to his wife, twenty days after his arrival in Tahiti, he wrote: 'I have already seen so many new things that I am quite unsettled. I shall need some further time before I can paint a good picture' (Malingue *Letters*, 1948, p. 162).
    Then, in 1903, he reminisced about his arrival in Arles in 1888 and compared himself to other

painters who can get off a train anywhere, pick up their palette and knock off an effect of sunlight instantly – there was no love lost between Gauguin and Impressionism. 'I don't admire the painting', he wrote, 'but I admire the man – so sure of himself and serene, whereas I am so uncertain and anxious.'

He concludes: 'In each locale I need a period of incubation, to learn each time the particular character of the plants, the trees – of the whole landscape, so varied and capricious, never wanting to leave herself vulnerable to being understood' (*Avant et Après*, pp. 9–10).

31   Gauguin had a large collection of prints, photographs and reproductions with him in Tahiti – 'a little community of comrades' as he called them. They ranged from Greek and Egyptian art to ancient Oriental art, Renaissance and Baroque painting, Japanese prints, contemporary French art and so on. They are often mentioned in his writings – especially in *Avant et Après* – and he pasted a few items into the *Diverses Choses* appendix to the Louvre MS. Richard Field's book contains the most useful discussion of the collection as source material for his art (Field 1977).

43   Van Gogh: drawing of a young woman. *c.*1888. Pen, pasted onto p. 205 of the Louvre MS

32   The detailed description of the Tahitian woman was another addition in the original manuscript: a separate sheet pasted in.

33   Gauguin left the Poe quotation incomplete in his manuscript, as if he was interrupted while writing and forgot to complete it: it is on the reverse side of another pasted-in sheet of writing.
      In the Louvre MS (p. 46), it is completed: '*Il n'y a pas de beauté parfaite sans une certaine singularité dans les proportions.*' In the *Cahier pour Aline*, in a section headed '*Notes d'Edgar Poe*', Gauguin includes a more accurate version of the quotation: '*Il n'y a pas de beauté exquise sans quelque étrangeté dans les proportions.*'
      The source is Poe's *Ligeia*: '"There is no exquisite beauty", says Bacon, Lord Verulam, speaking truly of all the forms and *genera* of beauty, "without some strangeness in the proportion".'
      How appropriate to Gauguin not only that the 'original' should also be borrowed, but that it had already been slightly changed in the process. Francis Bacon had originally written: 'There is no excellent beauty that hath not some strangeness in the proportion' (*Essay on Beauty*, 1625).
      A thought of this kind, whatever the precise wording, was certain to find favour with Gauguin, dissatisfied as he was with accepted conventions of beauty, proportion, whatever. It was, after all, very much a thought of his time: not far from Baudelaire's 'the beautiful is always bizarre', which was itself fortified if not inspired by Poe's influence. The translation of Poe that Gauguin used was probably by Baudelaire.
      Morice mentions that Gauguin's most favoured authors were Balzac and Poe (Morice 1920, p. 42).

34   '*tane*' means man or husband.
      Gauguin had long admired Manet's painting. He painted his copy of it shortly after the Manet masterpiece entered the Luxembourg museum in 1890. According to Rotonchamp, he spent a week working in front of the original (Rotonchamp, *Gauguin*, 1925, pp. 82–3). Degas bought Gauguin's copy in 1895.
      Echoes of *Olympia* may be seen in several of Gauguin's Tahitian paintings, for instance *Te Arii Vahine* (Woman with Mangoes), 1896. In Gauguin's work generally we may also sense a formative sympathy with Manet's improvisatory attitude to the use of ready-made source materials.

35   *Vahine no te Tiare* (Woman with a Flower) (Plate 8) was the first of Gauguin's Tahitian paintings to be seen in Paris, at Boussod & Valadon, in the autumn of 1892. It was also shown in Copenhagen the following year, and again in Paris in the 1893 show at Durand-Ruel.
      The translation of the title is Gauguin's (*La Femme à la Fleur*). L. J. Bouge adds that *Tiare* is a type of gardenia (Wildenstein 1958, p. 164).

36   Gauguin wrote 'See B' in the manuscript at this point. See Note 19.

37   In the manuscript, the handwritten text of Chapters II and III is continuous. After the words '*Je m'en separai*' (I parted from her), a strong wavy line has been drawn across the page with the note 'Chapter II (the story-teller speaks) ends here'. The handwriting is not Gauguin's, but probably Morice's.
      (In the Louvre MS, the first words of our Chapter III – 'Alone again' – have been tacked onto the end of Chapter II instead. They make equally good sense in either place.)

38   There are several reflections in Gauguin's writing of his affection for Voltaire's *Candide*. In *Avant et Après*, he cites the book during a discussion of Rousseau and Voltaire (p. 189). Later in that MS, he quotes this same Pangloss line in a draft letter to two Government inspectors in Tahiti (p. 213).
      The moral of the anecdote about the village elder that Gauguin has just told is itself in the spirit of *Candide*. The image it gives of the Tahitian people corresponds with almost every contemporary European account: that they were relaxed and pleasure-loving, but with no sense of stamina or discipline.
      At the end of this section in the original manuscript, Gauguin wrote the words 'journey around the island'. The words were later struck out and the account of the journey does not appear until Chapter VI (p. 33).

44   Opposite top: Copy after Manet's *Olympia*. 1890/1. 89 × 130 cm. W413. Coll. Mme A. Bergh, Oslo

45   Opposite bottom: *Te Arii Vahine* (Woman with mangoes). s. & d. 1896. 97 × 130 cm. W542. Hermitage, Leningrad

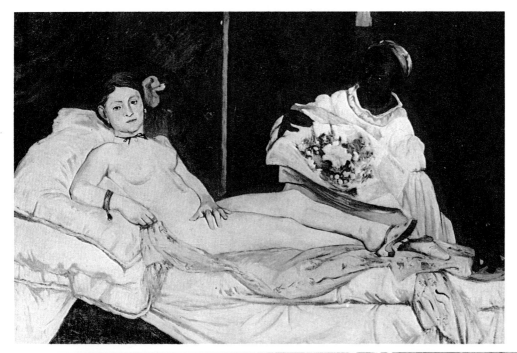

39 Jénot, the naval lieutenant who had met Gauguin the minute he stepped off the ship in Papeete, wrote later of the painter's problems with the language. 'The pupil had a distressing capacity for forgetting, for mixing syllables or for turning them upside down' (Wildenstein 1958, p. 118).

In March 1893, Gauguin wrote to de Monfried: 'I speak the Maori language pretty well now and find it very amusing' (Segalen, *Lettres*, 1950, p. 69).

In a more gloomy mood a month later, he paints a different picture to his wife: 'In the evenings I study the language a little, I have such a bad memory' (Malingue, *Letters*, 1948, p. 180).

40 The mention here of 'naked feet' is symbolic of wider issues. He writes later about the invidious influence of Europe on Marquesan culture:

> The child who is kept in school, deprived of physical exercise, his body always clad (for the sake of decency) becomes delicate and incapable of enduring a night in the mountains. They are all beginning to wear shoes and their feet, which are tender now, cannot cope with the rough paths or the sharp stones in the streams . . . we are witnessing the extinction of a race . . .

(*Avant et Après*, p. 53)

41 By 'Indian', Gauguin here means simply 'native' or 'primitive'.

42 Alongside this passage in the manuscript, Gauguin made the following notes:

1 The androgynous aspect of the savage, the slight difference of sex among animals——

2 The purity of thought associated with the sight of naked bodies and the relaxed behaviour between the two sexes——

Vice unknown among the savages——
Desire to be for a moment weak, a woman . . .

The separation of this note into a box alongside the text is unusual in the MS. It is not an afterthought; he was clearly aware from the outset that an explanatory argument needed further development, to complement the narrative. Possibly, as Loize suggests, he was also particularly anxious not to be misunderstood on this point.

The notes are developed in the Louvre MS (pp. 79–80) into a long comparison of the exaggerated distinction between the sexes in Western culture (fashion, corsetry, etc.) with the natural, egalitarian near-nakedness that was the norm in Polynesia. The passage emphasizes the synthetic triviality that attends the moral and sexual codes of Europe.

The desirability of an affinity between the sexes is a recurrent theme in Gauguin's writing. As early as 1888, he advised Madeleine Bernard to become an '*Androgyne*' (Malingue, *Letters*, 1948, p. 103). In Tahiti, he found confirmation of his instincts.

Victor Segalen describes Maori women as having essentially the build of a young man: 'broad shoulders . . . slight hips . . . naturally androgynous' (Segalen, *Lettres*, 1950, p. 27). The Louvre MS observes that in Europe, by comparison, 'our women have nothing in common with us and this may not be without grave moral and social disadvantages.' It seems very likely that such a passage was written after discussion between the two collaborators, on the strength of the notes in the Draft MS.

Andersen (1971) and Field (1977) have broached the question of the personal significance of Gauguin's championship of the androgynous condition. Relevant issues in Gauguin's biography may be his very close identifications with his grandmother, Flora Tristan, and his mother; as well as his bitter conflicts with his wife over male/female roles. (Incidentally, when Gauguin first arrived in Tahiti, he was dubbed *taata vahine* (man-woman) by the natives, because of his picturesque hat and the shoulder length of his salt-and-pepper hair (Jénot, in Wildenstein 1958, p. 117).)

Relevant clues in his art may be his obsessive concern with the goddess Hina (elevated by Gauguin out of all proportion to her place in Maori hierarchies), the sometimes ambiguous nature of her representation; and, more clearly, the explicitly androgynous nature of the *Oviri* image, which Gauguin wanted to stand on his tomb (Segalen, *Lettres*, 1950, p. 165). He refers to the image variously as 'monster', 'murderess' and 'this strange figure, cruel enigma'. (Plates 78, 79)

43 The phrase 'answering my previous desire' was only included in the Draft MS as an afterthought, giving the second meaning to Gauguin's cry of 'Oh no'.

Lower down the page there is another addition. The penultimate paragraph, from the words 'In time with the noise of the axe . . .' down to the end of the three lines of verse, was added as a footnote in the manuscript.

46 *Tahitian mountains. c.*1891. 68 × 92 cm. W504. Institute of Arts, Minneapolis

Finally, at the very end of this story, he added the words *'un parfum'* (a fragrance) to the final sentence.

44 Danielsson (1966, pp. 109, 299 n.79) suggests that Gauguin made this trip into the island's mountainous centre during a stay in Paea in 1892, when, without money, he was obliged to take a brief casual job as caretaker of a second-hand furniture store. Geographically this makes sense: the Punaru river that he mentions meets the coast just north of Paea.

The Punaru is one of several rivers that have cut deep valleys down to the coast from the central mountains of Orohena and Arorai. The third mountain that Gauguin mentions, the Diadem, is an adjacent ridge described by Lafarge as 'a fantastic serrated peak' (1914, p. 307).

45 *tupapau* = spirits of the dead

46 According to Moerenhout (Vol. I, p. 409), the tree *bouraao* is a type of hibiscus. In giving the same meaning for the title of a painting of 1892, *Te Burao* (W486), J. L. Bouge explains that there is no 'B' in Tahitian and Gauguin should have written *Te Purao* or *Te Purau* (Wildenstein 1958, p. 163). Gauguin was by no means alone among Europeans in his varied spelling of Tahitian words. He has been taken to task for his spelling *'Mahorie'*, but this variant appears elsewhere as well – in Bovis (1855) for example.

47   *Pape Moë* = mysterious water.

Gauguin's note here 'Description of the picture *Pape Moë*' is followed up in the Louvre MS (p. 87) with this brief account of the painting's motif:

> Suddenly at an abrupt turning, I saw a naked young girl standing against the rock face which she seemed to be caressing more than holding on to. She drank from a gushing spring that fell a great distance among the rocks. When she had finished drinking . . .

One of the two poems for *Noa Noa* that Morice wrote between 1895 and 1897, and which Gauguin copied into the Louvre MS (p. 89) from *La Revue Blanche*, was also called *Pape Moë*. Translation of a few lines may give both the flavour and the relationship to Gauguin's imagery:

> Tahitian source! Purifying water! Sacred water!
> Source of truth, your brilliance enlightens me.
> . . . . O I shall drink
> from your sacred stream to purify my heart,
> And then I want to wash my hands, my head, my lips
> to heal them from the burning of malign fevers,
> And I want to wash my eyes in order to see
> The ancient way of life reflected in your mirror,
> . . . .

See also p. 114 for the source of the image. (Plates 14, 73, 74)

48   Mount Arorai is the centre of the island, not easy to reach and possibly an achievement of Gauguin's imagination, but also a useful literary device by which to change focus onto a Maori legend! In the Louvre MS (p. 88), the transition is manoeuvred thus:

> Not without difficulty and fatigue, I at last arrived close to Arorai; the summit of the Isle, the dreaded mountain. It was evening and the moon was rising. Watching it, I was reminded of that sacred dialogue in the very place where legend tells us it was first performed.

The sacred dialogue that follows (Louvre MS, pp. 88–9) is quoted very closely from Moerenhout (1837, Vol. I, pp. 428–9) via Gauguin's *Ancien Culte Mahorie* (pp. 13ff).

> Hina said to Téfatou:
> Make man live again after his death.
> The God of the Earth replied to the Goddess of the Moon:
> – No I shall not revive him.
> Man will die, the vegetation will die, as will those that live from it, the earth will die,
> the earth will be finished, finished never to be reborn.
>
> Hina replied
> Do what you will. As for me, I shall revive the *Moon*.
>
> And that which was Hina's continued to be, and that which was Téfatou's perished, and man must die.

49   The meaning of the phrase 'I was short of many documents' is not clear either from this literal translation or from Gauguin's biography. It is documentation or source material that he refers to.

In a letter of March 1892, he wrote to de Monfried: 'I am working harder and harder, but so far only on studies, or rather in documents, which are building up – If they are not useful to me later they will be to others' (Segalen, *Lettres*, 1950, p. 54). This has properly been interpreted as reference to his researches from Moerenhout's book, i.e. the compiling of the *Ancien Culte Mahorie*. His often-quoted letter to Sérusier ('What a religion. . . . What a marvel!') dates from the same month. Field (1977) argues convincingly that Gauguin's discovery of Moerenhout precipitated a breakthrough in his Tahitian painting early in 1892.

Perhaps Gauguin's implication that his work was suffering because of a lack of source material is a retrospective reconstruction of his feelings of disappointment and frustration during the early months in Tahiti – before he was introduced to Moerenhout's book?

50   'divorced for some months' refers to his separation from Titi.

51 Anani was the man in Mataiea from whom Gauguin had rented his bamboo hut, and who at one point nursed him through illness.

A painting on the glass panels of a door, *Woman with Fruit* (W552), has been assigned to this period by some writers who believe that it was painted for Anani's house (Danielsson, 1966, pp. 94–7, 110). The painting was bought later by Somerset Maugham.

52 Maybe, like the fictitious 'small valley', this plunge into the mountains is also a fiction. Danielsson's supposition that Gauguin took the coast road from Mataiea to Taravao seems reasonable – it was the only route used by public transport and his next stop, Faaone, is a little further round the coast.

The invention of this interlude allowed him to introduce a description of two of the paintings that *Noa Noa* had originally set out to explain.
(See Note 53)

53 The motif of *Hina Maruru* (Thanks to Hina) is like a detail of the other painting he mentions, *Matamua/Autrefois* (W467) (Plates 91 and 72).

The expanded text of this section in the Louvre MS (pp. 98–9) is loosely based on the two paintings. The natives of this imagined valley, where life went on within Maori traditions, lived out Gauguin's dream:

> They were happy and calm. They dreamt, they loved, they slept, they sang, they prayed, and I could see clearly – even though they weren't there – the statues of their female gods. Statues of Hina and fêtes in honour of this Goddess of the Moon . . .

> Around her people danced the rituals of times past – *matamua* – and the *vivo's* note varies from clear and gay to sombre and melancholic according to the hour of day.

(See also p. 114)

54 Morice, with a sense of propriety that informs his editing from time to time, added a note in parentheses to the 1901 *La Plume* version of *Noa Noa* that the age of thirteen in a Maori girl was equivalent to eighteen or twenty years in a European girl. It has become almost a tradition among later writers to repeat this information.

55 The correct Maori spelling of Tehamana would be Teha'amana, meaning 'giver of strength' (Danielsson 1966, p. 119). In the Louvre MS and all subsequent editions of *Noa Noa*, the name was altered to Tehura, sometimes Téhura, for no obvious reason (easier to get the tongue around, Danielsson suggests).

The misspelling of the name as 'Tehaurana' throughout the 1961 English translation appears to have been a simple misreading of the manuscript.

56 The indented phrase 'Maori character . . . French character' is encircled in Gauguin's manuscript as if earmarked for further development. In the Louvre MS (pp. 105–6) the theme is extended as follows:

> In this way, very much at my own expense, I learnt the sort of profound lesson that distinguishes an Oceanian soul from that of a European, most of all a Frenchman. The Maori character does not reveal itself straightaway: it demands great patience and application to even begin to understand it.

> It escapes you at first and can disconcert you in a thousand ways, disguised by laughter and by their gift for transformation.

> Just when I thought I had the measure both of her outward appearance and of her inner moods, she could – without a thought of putting on an act – confront me with an untroubled self-assurance that was carefree, mocking and childishly frivolous.

This character-sketch of the Tahitian corresponds to a normal European visitor's reaction: it is echoed in different ways by Bovis (1855), Johnstone (1905), Lafarge (1914) and Best (1924).
Gauguin's Story of the Ear-rings (p. 53) is a continuation of the same theme.

57 This italicized part of the sentence is underlined in Gauguin's manuscript, probably to draw attention to the need for rewriting; although in the event, it remains unaltered in the Louvre MS, apart from the addition of the word 'But' at the start of the sentence. This makes clearer the slightly veiled meaning of the phrase. The sense is that the moving radiance of Tehamana's body sometimes expressed the love that she never spoke of.

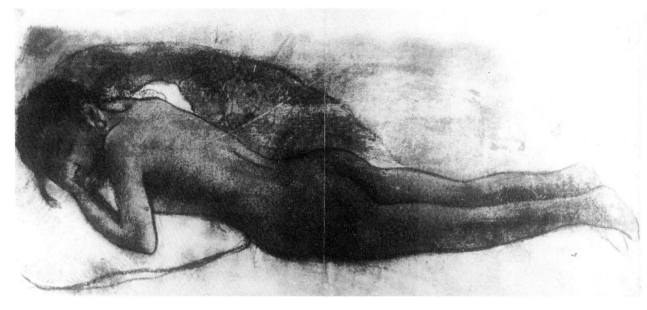

47 Reclining nude. *c.*1892. Charcoal. Present whereabouts unknown

58 As an example of the chorus-like refrain which is used in the Louvre MS, this passage is rendered there (p. 107) as follows:

> And the Eve of this Paradise lets herself become more and more docile and loving. I am bathed in her fragrance: *Noa Noa*!

59 The section on the legend of Roua and the birth of the stars is taken verbatim from Moerenhout (Vol. II, pp. 206–11), *Ancien Culte Mahorie* (pp. 38–42).
   In the manuscript, the section is added on a separate sheet of paper, pasted onto page 20, suggesting perhaps that the decision to use material from *Ancien Culte Mahorie* may have followed the initial conception of *Noa Noa*.

60 As Loize has pointed out (1966, p. 119n), 'Tauroua' is one of many examples of confusion over spelling of names in the successive transcriptions, first from Moerenhout into the *Ancien Culte Mahorie* and from there into the several MSS of *Noa Noa* by Gauguin and by Morice.
   In *Ancien Culte Mahorie*, Gauguin spelt the morning star as *Tauroua* and the King as *Fauroua*; subsequently both as *Tauroua*. In Moerenhout, it is clear that both should be *Fauroua*!

61 This refers to the painting *Manao Tupapau* (Plate 16). Gauguin's detailed explanations of it are well known from the 'Birth of a Painting' section of *Cahier pour Aline* and from his letters of December 1892. Field (1977, pp. 108ff) undertakes a careful critical analysis of Gauguin's explanations.
   In the Louvre MS (p. 109), there is an extended rather melodramatic addition to the account given here.

> Motionless, naked, lying face down on the bed, her eyes immeasurably larger from fear, Tehura looked at me and seemed not to know me. I too was caught for several moments by a strange feeling of uncertainty. Tehura's terror was contagious. I had the illusion that a phosphorescent light was streaming from her staring eyes. Never had I seen her so beautiful, so frighteningly beautiful . . .

This fragment illustrates the sort of rewriting that is traditionally – and not unreasonably – laid at Morice's door.
   The painting is one that Gauguin valued very highly; it is clearly one of the major works of the first Tahitian period. It exemplifies first of all the impact of Moerenhout's book on his subject-matter. Secondly it is a classic example of the fusion of reality and fiction of his mature work. Formally it brings together a study from life with invented images. Its content brings together a remembered incident with imaginative notions of Maori spirits. The two accounts of Tehura's reaction – that she

48 Top: *The Meal* (The bananas). s. & d. 1891. 73 × 92 cm. W427. Louvre (Jeu de Paume), Paris

49 Wooden bowl carved by Gauguin. *c.*1891. Tamanu wood, 1.44 cm. Gray 145. Louvre (Jeu de Paume), Paris

was haunted by the *tupapau*, the spirits of the dead, and that she was angrily suspicious that Gauguin had been with prostitutes in Papeete – pose a similar confrontation between fiction and probable truth.

Loize (1966, p. 120) links Tehura's mention of women 'who go to the market' with Gauguin's painting *Ta Matete* (Plate 3), an image of finely dressed women seated on a bench while the activity of the market goes on behind them.

62   The Story of the Ear-rings (p. 53) is slotted into the Louvre MS at this point.

63   It has been suggested that Gauguin had seen tattooing in Tahiti (Loize/Griffin 1961, p. 40), but this seems unlikely.

Jénot recalls that 'Gauguin showed me photographs of Marquesans wholly or partly covered in tattoos whose design he admired' (Wildenstein 1958, p. 121). Where the photographs came from we cannot be certain, maybe from Tahiti, maybe from New Zealand en route, maybe even from Paris, at the Exposition Universelle of 1889, where he had picked up photographs of Javanese art for instance (Malingue, *Letters*, 1948, p. 118).

It is not clear from the literature what was the prevailing practice of tattooing in Tahiti in the 1890s, if any. The custom was discouraged in other parts of Polynesia and had always been less prevalent and less spectacular in Tahiti than elsewhere.

The Marquesan rubbings that Gauguin pasted into the Louvre MS (Plates 53, 55) are very close in style to Marquesan tattoos. Gauguin's own carving (Plate 49) was in some respects closely based on Marquesan decoration, long before he settled in the Marquesas in 1901. One can readily appreciate the affinity that he felt with craftsmen who decorated anything that was to hand.

'One is astonished to find a face where one thought there was nothing but a strange geometric figure', he writes. 'Always the same thing and yet never the same' (*Avant et Après*, pp. 49ff).

64   In an undated letter to William Molard (?summer 1895), Gauguin writes: 'Please tell Charles Morice to change words in the book *Noa Noa* for me: the word "Bishop" should be replaced by "a clerical notable" in the story of the wedding' (Loize 1966, p. 82). If the message ever got through, it was ignored or forgotten; the Bishop was still included in the 1901 *La Plume* edition.

Did he wish not to disturb his own peaceful co-existence with the Protestant church in Tahiti any more than necessary? This is hardly in character, but on the other hand this chapter is almost certainly an objective account of a real event.

The ironic, slightly gossipy, nod-and-wink style of the conclusion is very characteristic of Gauguin's commentaries on contemporary Tahiti. Much of *Avant et Après* is written in this style and it appears in a rather more acid form in his articles for *Les Guêpes* and *La Sourire* (Danielsson & O'Reilly 1966).

65   This whole chapter is another mixture of real experience and a legend lifted intact from Moerenhout – each of them embroidered a little. The fishing expedition obviously happened: the legend of Rouahatou and Tehamana's prayer are borrowed; the superstition about infidelity was most likely passed on to Gauguin by word of mouth, maybe even in the way he describes. (We may reasonably doubt, however, that Gauguin was thinking of the Buddha on the 'tropical night'.) Danielsson claims to have found witnesses to Tehamana's 'infidelities' (1966, p. 300 n.92).

66   The legend of Rouahatou is taken verbatim from Moerenhout (I, pp. 573–4), via *Ancien Culte Mahorie* (pp. 36–7).

67   The prayer credited to Tehamana is taken directly from Moerenhout (II, pp. 81–3). Moerenhout cites it as an example of the prayers recited, *sotto voce* and in unison, at the end of an evening gathering in Tahiti.

In *Ancien Culte Mahorie*, it appears under the heading '*Une Prière Maorie*' (pp. 51–2).

68   The sentence 'Naked like that . . . Bhixu' was added as a footnote in the manuscript. So too was the quotation from Buddha in the next paragraph.

69   In the original manuscript, page 28, the word '*finement*' (subtly) is a correction from what was first written – '*finalement*'. Alterations like this suggest that Gauguin's Draft MS was – in part at least – copied from earlier notes. The mistake is that of the copyist misreading the word, rather than of someone having second thoughts about the meaning.

70   This talk of 'imperative family duties' is pure window dressing. Gauguin had started applying for repatriation – for financial reasons above all other – as early as summer 1892. It is true that when he last saw his wife he talked in terms of them being 'remarried' on his return and later of re-establishing the family, maybe even of the whole family starting life together in the tropics. But these issues were not the reason for his return and he did not see his family again.

   The family issue that most engaged him on his return to Paris was the death of his uncle Isidore in Orléans, from whose estate he inherited a sum approaching 10,000 francs.

   In the Louvre MS, this last chapter is entitled 'The storyteller concludes his tale' (p. 203).

   Gauguin left Tahiti on June 14th, 1893 and arrived in Marseilles on August 30th (Danielsson 1966, pp. 140–4).

71   In fact Gauguin had seen 'this old Maori saying' on page 413 of Moerenhout's first volume and had copied it into pages 52–3 of *Ancien Culte Mahorie*.

   The word *'fin'* is written at the foot of the quotation in the manuscript, not in Gauguin's hand, maybe in Morice's. In the Louvre MS and subsequent versions of *Noa Noa*, the text does end here.

72   This Appendix does not appear in any other version of *Noa Noa*. The decision to omit it should not come as a surprise. It is not simply that its structure is casual and inconclusive. Gauguin's complaints about the obstructive role played by the French authorities before, during and after his stay in Tahiti represent a sub-plot that could only detract from the fragrance of *Noa Noa*. Its contents contribute nothing to *Noa Noa*'s purpose and stand to overbalance the primitive/European axis around which *Noa Noa* was built. After trying the material first at the beginning of his manuscript and then at the end, this was obviously Gauguin's (and/or Morice's) conclusion as well. The best sources of detailed information on this sub-plot are Danielsson (1966) and *Avant et Après*.

73   The Monsieur 'D' referred to was a painter, Louis-Jules Dumoulin.

   As part of his mission, Gauguin was verbally promised the purchase of at least one of his works for 3,000 francs, but on his return, the Director of the Beaux Arts, Ronjon, refused to encourage an art that he could not understand and challenged Gauguin to produce any written agreement. When, in a state of illness and poverty in 1896, Gauguin received from the Directorate the sum of 200 francs 'by way of encouragement', he sent it back (Morice 1920, p. 93; *Avant et Après*, pp. 181–2).

74   Danielsson (1966, pp. 140ff) gives details of the four government departments involved in the delay over Gauguin's repatriation.

75   Gauguin omits to mention here that he did *not* travel third class all the way home from Noumea. He spent the last of his money to transfer to second class (Segalen, *Lettres*, 1950, p. 75).

76   The abrupt break in the text here perhaps suggests some dissatisfaction on Gauguin's part with the direction the Appendix was taking.

77   Because this story is inserted somewhat abruptly into the Louvre MS as an interlude in the chapter on Maori mythology, it is prefaced by the following justification (p. 138):

   But all of this is very long and arduous to listen to – let us pause – It will not matter – to branch out our story in a different direction will help understanding of the work as a whole – Allow me then to interrupt with this account of a walk with Tehura –

78   The *taro* is a tropical plant of the arum family with tuberous roots, much used in Polynesian cooking.

79   *Toe toe* means 'too cold'.

80   Morea should read Moorea, a slip of Gauguin's pen. (See Note 3.)

The facts and fictions
of Noa Noa

I   The history of Noa Noa

Gauguin's first stay in Tahiti was between June 1891 and June 1893. He arrived back in Paris at the end of August 1893 ('two years older and twenty years younger', as he told Morice) and in November–December 1893 exhibited his Tahitian paintings for the first time, at Durand-Ruel's gallery. 'I shall soon know whether or not it was an act of lunacy to go to Tahiti', he wrote to his wife.[1]

For his own reasons he later wrote to tell her what a resounding artistic success it had been – 'For the moment I am considered by many people to be the greatest modern painter'[2] – but if success or failure of his Tahitian expedition were to be measured by the show at Durand-Ruel, then the verdict was at best unclear. Of the forty-four paintings and two carvings exhibited only eleven paintings were sold, barely covering his expenses. Critical response was by no means all favourable: Gauguin himself later recalled that 'the critics howled before my canvases, saying they were too dense, too non-dimensional'.[3] As far as artists were concerned, Degas was among the purchasers, but Pissarro wrote to his son: 'Only Degas admires, Monet and Renoir find this simply bad. I saw Gauguin . . . I told him that his art did not belong to him, that he was a civilized man and hence it was his function to show us harmonious things. We parted both unconvinced . . . Everyone to whom I talked about Gauguin's exhibition was furious. . . . They are all even more outraged than me.'[4]

In the same letters, however, Pissarro did mention the enthusiasm of 'all men of letters'. This was Morice's circle: the same circle of Symbolist writers, presided over by Mallarmé, who had largely made up the guest list at the farewell banquet for Gauguin two years before.[5] Morice had written the catalogue essay for Gauguin's 1893 exhibition, and at some point during the build-up to that show the *Noa Noa* project must first have been floated. In the two letters to his wife quoted above, he writes that 'I am also preparing a book on Tahiti' and of 'a book about my voyage which is causing me a lot of hard work'. De Monfried recalls Gauguin giving readings from a written account of the Tahitian trip to him in his studio in 1893.[6] There is no record of what this material was, although it is reasonable to assume from the alleged date that it was taken from Gauguin's Draft MS. Jean Loize concludes – following de Monfried but with no other substantiation – that Gauguin originated all of this material and only afterwards showed it to Morice.[7]

Morice says later, quite categorically, that it was his idea first.[8] What is probable is that by the end of 1893 Gauguin's first draft was completed; written largely from memory, but partly from notes, some of which he brought back with him from Tahiti.[9] Its increasingly fragmented form, with notes of subjects to be developed and paintings to be described, etc., makes clear Gauguin's intention to rewrite. We may assume that from the outset this rewriting was to be done in collaboration with Morice. Morice

50 p. 82: *Merahi Metua No Tehamana* (Tehamana has many ancestors). s. & d. 1893. 75 × 53 cm. W497. Coll. Institute of Arts, Chicago

51 Opposite: *Noa Noa*. Cover of 1924 Crès edition, illustrated with woodcuts after Gauguin by Daniel de Monfried

52 Left: Engraved reproduction of Gauguin's *Ia Orana Maria* of 1891, partly retouched with watercolour, pasted onto p. 125 of the Louvre MS

53 Rubbing from Marquesan carved ornament. Pencil and watercolour, 12.5 × 13 cm. Pasted onto p. 126 of the Louvre MS

writes that he contributed all of the narrative chapters from Gauguin's notes and submitted them for Gauguin's approval.[10] The notes that we know Morice worked from were the Draft MS and Gauguin's small illustrated Tahitian notebook, *Ancien Culte Mahorie*, which will be discussed in detail later.[11]

The Draft MS remained in Morice's possession and subsequently 'disappeared' for about sixty years. We now know that in October 1908 Morice wrote to a print dealer, Edmond Sagot: 'I possess a Gauguin manuscript of exceptional interest. It is in a *cahier* of more than thirty pages, large format, the first draft of notes from which I made – in *Noa Noa* – the account of Gauguin's first stay in Tahiti. These pages are without doubt and uniquely from Gauguin's hand. You will understand the importance of such a document . . .' Sagot bought it and it was his heirs who published a facsimile edition (including Morice's letter) in 1954.[12] When the manuscript was sold, several draft pages of *Noa Noa* in Gauguin's hand were not included.[13] Morice published one page in the 1920 edition of his monograph.[14] It appears likely that Gauguin drafted other material for *Noa Noa* as well whose manuscripts have disappeared.[15] Around April 1894, Gauguin wrote to Morice that he had 'just finished his graphic work *(gravure)* on *Noa Noa*. This will contribute greatly to the book's success: so it is crucial that the book is made – and very soon.'[16] This is a reference to the ten large woodcuts, all of related subjects: *Te Po, Noa Noa, Manao Tupapau, Te Faruru, Maruru, Nave Nave Fenua, Te Atua, Mahna no Varua ino, Auti te Pape, l'Univers est créé*. Loize suggests that Gauguin may have had in mind a separate album of prints as a supplement to the book. The blocks are certainly very large for a book. Their height is enough to fill the Louvre MS pages with no margin. (See Plates 1, 4, 31, 32, 33, 54, 82, 91, 101.)

In April 1894, Gauguin left Paris for Pont Aven, in Brittany. He stayed there until mid-November, largely because of an incident at Concarneau when local children shouted abuse at Gauguin's diminutive mistress Anna the Javanese and her monkey, and a vicious brawl with a group of sailors followed. According to Gauguin, he took on fifteen men single-handed until he fell and was kicked brutally with wooden clogs.[17] He suffered a broken and dislocated ankle and was bedridden for at least two months.[18] Loize suggests that at this time Gauguin wrote out his copy of the collaborative text, i.e. the Louvre MS. He quotes a fragment of a letter of June 1st, 1894 in which Gauguin exclaims: 'Unbelievable Morice! I must have the copied manuscript (I don't mean mine). It was finished!!! It remained only for you to add the few unwritten verses . . . Now there can be nothing to do . . .'[19] Ambiguous though it is, the fragment at least makes clear that a version later than his own draft existed before Gauguin left Paris in April 1894.

Gauguin was unable to paint during his convalescence and if he did receive the manuscript asked of Morice, Loize's hypothesis that he copied it out while bedridden seems reasonable. Some of the watercolour illustrations to the Louvre MS were

54 *Te Atua* (The Gods). c.1894/5. Woodcut, 20.5 × 35.5 cm. Guérin 31. Museum of Modern Art, New York

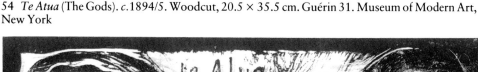

obviously made at the same time as or before the copying out, since the words are written around the image.[20] Some fifty pages were left blank to accommodate the missing Morice material, some with notes about what was to come (e.g. at Chapter III 'A group of six poems to come. Five in verse, one in prose';[21] and at Chapter IX *(Nave Nave Fenua)* Gauguin copies out: 'Small images with large frames. Lyrical episodes. Nature illuminates the legends. Prose and verse. To come!'.[22] There was also some discussion of drawings for *Noa Noa* made in Brittany and given to Morice on Gauguin's return to Paris. Morice later complains that their quality was unsuitable for reproduction.[23]

After two years in France, neither particularly happy nor successful and which only strengthened him in his resolve that 'Western life is futile', Gauguin returned to Tahiti in the summer of 1895. The last months in France were very busy, not least with preparation for another fund-raising exhibition and sale of his work. We do not know a great deal about progress on *Noa Noa* at this point: probably there was not much. Early in the year, Morice informed Gauguin that 'I have a complete manuscript of our *Noa Noa*'[24] and this may be confirmed by the date 1895 on one of the two manuscripts in Morice's possession at his death.[25] It is unlikely that Gauguin saw it. He did not add to his own copy of the manuscript at this time, although he did write to William Molard on arrival in Tahiti: 'It seems that *Noa Noa* will appear.'[26] Even so, before Gauguin left Paris, he had assigned to this same friend, Molard, the power of attorney to act on his behalf in any negotiations concerning publication.[27]

It appears that Gauguin left in Morice's care not only his Draft MS but also the *Ancien Culte Mahorie* notebook – there is some disagreement on this point[28] – and that Morice completed work on a further revision by 1897. The second manuscript of *Noa Noa* among Morice's papers at his death in 1919 was dated 1897[29] and it was later that year that two substantial excerpts were published in *La Revue Blanche* in Paris.

By this time, Gauguin's faith in the publication was waning rapidly. In December 1895 he wrote to a friend: 'Speaking of Morice, I see that *Noa Noa* has reached the very bottom of the pit'[30] and, at the end of a bitter letter to Morice on the subject of unpaid debts, May 1896: 'Think of all this Morice and remember that actions speak louder than words.'[31]

In March 1897 Morice wrote to Gauguin about a possible illustrated edition of *Noa Noa* suggesting – since his drawings would not reproduce well because of their coarse-grained paper – that 'an artist who understands you – Séguin for example' might make new versions of them for publication.[32] In September Morice wrote again: 'On the 5th of next month, *Noa Noa* will start to appear in *La Revue Blanche*. All of your text will be published; only fragments of my poems . . . Do you agree to allow me half of the fee for author's copyright on publication in the review and on the first edition of this work?'[33]

Gauguin was incensed, writing to de Monfried: 'Go to the Director of *La Revue Blanche* and find out what are the fees . . . above all ask him to pay nothing to Morice . . . but to me as soon as possible and to prevent any money falling into Morice's hands.'[34] And then a month later: 'I have received a copy of *La Revue Blanche* with the first instalment of *Noa Noa*, but of course no money . . . Publication in reviews, as in newspapers, is normally paid for as soon as the issue appears. With books it is different, but I believe that as soon as the book is sold the author gets paid. If by chance – *and this is quite possible* – the book is going to be adapted as a document or published, I don't want my wife to have access to the profits.'[35] To Morice he wrote simply, 'Most likely I shall never see the book published, since my days are numbered.'[36]

The excerpts that appeared in *La Revue Blanche*[37] were introduced with this

55 Rubbings from Marquesan carved ornament. Pencil and watercolour, pasted onto p. 168 of the
Louvre MS

56 Right: Landscape with figure. 1897/1903? Watercolour, 30 × 22 cm. Louvre MS, p. 177
(see Plate 57)

57 *Landscape with a pig and a horse.* s. & d. 1903. 75 × 65 cm. W637. Art Museum of the Ateneum, Helsinki

paragraph, probably drafted by Morice: 'The pages that Mr Paul Gauguin and Mr Charles Morice devote to Tahiti have their point of departure in the paintings brought back from the island by Mr Gauguin. But it is not necessary to have seen the pictorial work to understand the literary work, of which we give you a first fragment today. What you will find here is not art criticism, but narrations – and other things beside.' In the event it was almost all narration in both excerpts: fragments of three Morice poems, a new prose and verse section by Morice, and all of Gauguin's texts apart from the chapter on Maori mythology. In addition, in the second instalment, Morice had inserted a further Gauguin text. In January 1897, Gauguin had written to him enclosing a fierce diatribe against the French colonial authorities in the form of an invented interview between Gauguin and a native. 'If you manage to have this published in a newspaper', Gauguin wrote, 'send me a few copies. I'd like to show a few skunks out here that I've still got some clout.'[38] Morice edited it, and slotted it into *Noa Noa*, quite out of any context, under the heading 'Note'.[39]

On receiving the October 15th issue of *La Revue Blanche*, Gauguin copied into the Louvre MS two of Morice's poems that had been missing in 1894: '*Vivo*' and '*Pape Moë*'.[40] He received no further material, nor any reassuring information about publication. The last page of text in the Louvre MS, page 346, is inscribed '*fin de volume – Janvier 1898*' and it is reasonably assumed that by the end of 1897 he had abandoned hope of receiving the outstanding material from Morice and started to fill up the reserved blank pages with drawings, photographs, etc.

His failed suicide attempt was probably very early in January 1898: he refers to it as 'last month' in a February letter to de Monfried. In the same letter,[41] he writes: 'Morice tells me that the book is no longer published by *La Revue Blanche*, but will probably be taken up by Charpentier, which is much better from the standpoint of publicity and therefore of money. I hope you are taking an interest in it and doing everything necessary. Who knows whether this book may not give me a lift and help my painting. At least it will not do me any harm.'

A month later this brief glimmer of optimism was gone. To de Monfried again: 'To come to *La Revue Blanche*, I don't understand anything about it. I received one number containing the beginning and then nothing: in this way it has neither head nor tail and the money to be had from it will be almost nothing, if it hasn't gone already.'[42] In the same month he wrote to Molard: 'Do not lose sight of the fact, my dear Molard, in spite of your preoccupations, that I have left you a special power of attorney for the publication of *Noa Noa*, which is always hanging fire with Morice. Keep this in mind, as otherwise, with this rascal, the money will slip through his fingers.'[43]

We know little more of anything happening in 1898. This is the period to which Loize ascribes a 'random' filling-up of blank pages in the Louvre MS, but this process may well have taken place over a drawn-out period. A series of watercolour landscapes among the pasted-in illustrations offers an example of the confusing evidence.[44] In character and topography they are closer to Gauguin's very last Martinique paintings than to the Tahitian landscapes of 1898–9. One of them, apart from the substitution of a horse for a figure and the introduction of a small defecating pig, is an almost verbatim replica of the painting *Landscape with a pig and a horse* (Plates 56, 57), signed and dated 1903, in other words from the very last months of Gauguin's life. This means at least that *Noa Noa* was still very much a part of his life until the end. Either in his bedridden state he was using the album as a source book for the motifs of paintings, or he was still filling in blank pages with some of his very last watercolours.[45] He certainly continued to discuss *Noa Noa* in correspondence with de Monfried as late as May 1902.[46]

To return to the dependable history: the next important letter, usually but not

58 p. 57 of the Louvre MS. Above left: Hina and Tefatou (fragment of the woodcut *Te Atua*,
see Plate 54). Above right: photograph of a Tahitian girl wearing a cross. Below: watercolour of Hiro
(see Plate 59)

Hiro (Dieu des voleurs) faisait avec ses doigts des trous dans les rochers. Il délivra une vierge retenue dans un lieu enchanté, gardée par des géans. Il arracha d'une seule main les arbres qui tenaient le lieu enchanté. Le charme fut rompu.

Ceinture Rouge (Symbole de la divinité et du feu.

59 Illustrations to the story of Hiro, god of thieves. c. 1892. Pen and watercolour. Size of page 22.5 × 18 cm. Ancien Culte Mahorie MS, p. 17

securely dated February 1899, is written in a spirit of total and final resignation about the future of *Noa Noa* and with serious reservations about the book's format and original intention. It is an incomplete letter; the addressee was simply 'madame', probably Mme Morice.[47] The relevant section reads as follows:

> The book *Noa Noa* is another matter. I beg of you to believe that I have a modicum of the experience and the instincts of a civilized person, savage though I am. The narrator need not disappear behind the poet. A book is what it is ... if by a few stories one says all that one has to say or to hint at, that is already a great deal. Verses are expected from Morice, I know, but if there should be many in this book, all of the narrator's naïveté would disappear and the flavour of *Noa Noa* would lose its origin. Aren't you afraid of those who are waiting jealously in the wings ... saying 'Yes Morice has talent, but he lacks creative inspiration and without Gauguin he would not have any ideas?' I am sure this will be said if there are too many poems. If on the other hand there were only a few poems, everything would fall into place and would realize the fine sequence that you know already exists in his manuscripts.
>
> Publication of his own volume immediately after being well introduced by *Noa Noa* would have far greater value ... Do not think for one moment that it is a question of *amour-propre* which leads me to say that if Morice wishes to publish the poems inspired by *Noa Noa* without the narrations and without any collaboration, then I give him full permission, happy to make the sacrifice for my friend. Let us say together to the little manuscript: 'Sleep. It is night. It is evening.'[48]

Loize interprets 'the little manuscript' to mean Gauguin's Draft MS.[49] The vagueness surrounding the letter unfortunately undermines any conclusions we might draw from it. It obviously implies unknown earlier exchanges between Gauguin and Morice and it is not difficult to associate Gauguin's explicit misgivings about the quantity of 'poems inspired by *Noa Noa*' with the long new section of prose and verse that Morice had written between 1895 and 1897.[50] Perhaps by the time he wrote this letter mooting a possible separation of their two contributions, Gauguin had after all seen the second instalment in *La Revue Blanche* and the extent to which Morice now had the collaborative-interpretative bit between his teeth.

Gauguin was in a calmer state generally by 1899 and in this letter he finally throws in the towel without the anguished urgency that had characterized most of his references to *Noa Noa*. In a similar tone in June 1899, he refused an invitation to exhibit with his Parisian peers of ten years ago explaining, 'My personality of ten years ago is of no interest today.'[51] It is a frame of mind with which we may easily associate the filling up of blank pages reserved for Morice with other material. The relationship between the added illustrations and the text of *Noa Noa* will be discussed later,[52] but the liberal way in which they are 'collaged' throughout the text links with the 'like dreams ... like life' quality of the final section of the Louvre MS, *Diverses Choses*.[53] This extraordinary miscellany of thoughts and images in its turn anticipates the character of his last manuscript *Avant et Après*,[54] which in some measure replaced *Noa Noa* in Gauguin's thinking.

In May 1901, Morice wrote to Gauguin with the news that, at last, 'I have just published *Noa Noa* at my own expense in a small book, very simple. I am sending you 100 copies ... let me know what you think of it. Its appearance is not very fine I know. ... But it is from the literary point of view that I should like your opinion. And could we not produce a sequel? You must have made more notes since your return to Tahiti. Think about it. I am at your service.'[55] Gauguin's first response was quiet and succinct: 'I confess that the publication of *Noa Noa* at quite the wrong time has no interest for me today. Why send me 100 copies? Out here they will be so much waste paper.'[56]

In the event, 100 copies were not sent and no subsequent correspondence on this subject between them has been published to date. In November 1901, shortly after his arrival in the Marquesas Islands, Gauguin wrote to de Monfried that '*Noa Noa* has been published without my knowledge. If you can get hold of a copy, send one to me.'[57] The following May, de Monfried mentions that he had asked Vollard to post one but doubts that he has.[58] Ironically, it seems likely that Gauguin never saw the published book.

The 1901 *La Plume* edition of Gauguin's text was largely the same as had appeared in *La Revue Blanche* four years earlier. Morice's contribution – minimal in *La Revue Blanche* – was considerable and very different from the Louvre MS. The *La Plume* version was, after all, the first appearance of the complete work that Morice had done on *Noa Noa* between 1895 and 1897, let alone any subsequent refinement. His introductory chapter ('*Songeries*' in the Louvre MS)[59] was extensively rewritten and re-titled '*Point de Vue*'. As well as the lyrical prose of the chapter '*Nave Nave Fenua*' by Morice that had appeared in *La Revue Blanche*, there were in all twenty-one poems, or – by Loize's calculation – 705 verses.[60]

Gauguin had written to de Monfried in November 1897: 'If I die suddenly I beg you to keep in memory of me all of the canvases that you are looking after: my family already has too many of them.'[61] After Gauguin's death, on May 8th, 1903, the Louvre MS arrived by a circuitous route into de Monfried's possession[62] and remained there (despite agitation from Gauguin's widow and the remaining children) until he presented it to the Louvre in 1925.[63]

In 1910, extracts of this version were published, with editorial comment on their distinctness from the *La Plume* text, in the magazine *Les Marges*.[64] The editor, Eugène Montfort, friend of de Monfried, wrote that it was simpler and more striking, that it had more flavour. Differences had been briefly noted in the first biography of Gauguin in 1906,[65] and from this point on the legend of Morice as the villain of the piece gathered momentum.

The history of *Noa Noa* is full of ironies. The first draft was wholly by Gauguin and the last version very largely written by Morice. Because of the reverse order in which the three principal versions became known to the public, it has seemed that Morice's participation was steadily pared away to reveal the 'authentic' original text within. After 1903, Morice was in the habit of signing copies of the *La Plume* edition as 'the survivor', but after that edition his name never again appeared as author. It is also ironic that just as Gauguin probably never saw Morice's *La Plume* edition, so Morice almost certainly did not see Gauguin's illustrated album, the Louvre MS.

Inevitably the history of the book is still littered with confusions. Gauguin's published correspondence is incomplete[66] and critical scholarship on any of Gauguin's writings is surprisingly limited. An example that gives some measure of the confusion is the disagreement between two of the most serious commentators, René Huyghe and Jean Loize, on the place and date of execution of the Louvre MS.[67] Huyghe's pioneer work on the *Ancien Culte Mahorie* was published in 1951, three years before publication of the rediscovered Draft MS. Loize's writings (1961 and 1966) had the advantage of a truer perspective of *Noa Noa*'s history.

Huyghe believes that Gauguin took a copy of the collaborative text with him to Tahiti and then copied it out again into the Louvre MS in 1896–7, and only at this stage made those watercolour illustrations that are painted directly onto the manuscript pages (rather than pasted in later). He suggests that Gauguin also took with him the *cahier, Ancien Culte Mahorie*, from which he copied ten of these earliest watercolours in the Louvre MS. Loize maintains they are not 'copies' from one to the other, but that both of them are from 'common sources' among Gauguin's notes and drawings. However, these common sources have not survived and the Louvre MS images have the detailed repetition that we associate with copies; in one case at least the size and silhouette are exact enough to suggest tracing.

Loize disagrees with Huyghe fundamentally. He believes that Gauguin had transcribed the collaborative text into the Louvre MS before he left France, during his convalescence in Pont Aven in 1894, and made all of the 'on-the-page' watercolours at that time. Finally, he believes that Morice retained possession of the *Ancien Culte Mahorie* at least until 1897 and continued to use it while drafting the final version of *Noa Noa*.

Further research on the second and third versions of *Noa Noa* may prove conclusively that Morice was still using the *Ancien Culte Mahorie* MS after Gauguin's return to Tahiti. If this were so, then Loize must be right. One point in favour of Huyghe's argument is that when Morice wrote in 1919 of the Louvre MS's origins he said, 'If later on in Tahiti or Dominique . . . Gauguin rewrote *Noa Noa* in his own hand and introduced some alterations to the original edition . . .', suggesting perhaps that the 'original edition' that Gauguin took back with him to Tahiti was *not* 'in his own hand'.[68] But as far as we know, no other version of *Noa Noa* was among Gauguin's papers at his death. What is more, since Morice had not seen the Louvre MS, he could only guess rather defensively what was in it. The field for conjecture remains open.

The three most contentious areas of confusion over *Noa Noa* relate to the evolving relationship between Gauguin and Morice, to judgements upon the originality and 'truth' of Gauguin's material, and finally to the purpose of the book. Although they bear upon each other, these three issues demand the separate consideration that follows.

Notes

1 Malingue, *Letters*, 1948, p. 187.
2 ibid, p. 188.
3 *Diverses Choses* (trans. *Writings of a Savage*, p. 137). See also *Cahier pour Aline*.
4 Pissarro, *Letters to Lucien*, 1943, pp. 221–2.
5 Danielsson, 1966, pp. 53–5.
6 Rotonchamp, 1906, p. 129.
7 Loize, 1966, p. 72; also Huyghe, 1951, p. 7.
8 Morice, 1920, pp. 187–8 n.
9 See Note 69 (p. 80).
10 Morice, 1920, p. 187.
11 See p. 109 ff.
12 Sagot – Le Garrec, Paris, 1954.
13 See p. 49 ff. (The Story of Princess Vaïtua).
14 Morice, 1920, p. 169. (See Pl. 60.)
15 See p. 48.
16 Loize, 1966, p. 76.
17 Malingue, *Letters*, 1948, p. 193.
18 See Perruchot, 1963, p. 257; Danielsson, 1966, p. 174.
19 Loize, 1966, p. 78.
20 Louvre MS, pp. 67, 75. (See Pls. 36, 100.)
21 ibid, p. 48.
22 ibid, p. 169.

23 Loize, 1966, p. 76.
24 ibid.
25 Letter from Mme Morice, August 1921. Loize, 1966, p. 100.
26 Malingue, *Letters*, 1948, p. 204.
27 ibid, p. 206.
28 See pp. 97–8.
29 Loize, 1966, p. 100.
30 Malingue, *Letters*, 1948, p. 204.
31 ibid, p. 206.
32 Loize, 1966, p. 83.
33 Segalen, *Lettres*, 1950, pp. 207–8.
34 ibid, p. 114.
35 ibid, p. 117.
36 Malingue, *Letters*, 1948, p. 209.
37 *La Revue Blanche*, Vol. XIV, 1897, pp. 81–103, 166–90.
38 Malingue, *Letters*, 1948, p. 209 (trans. *Writings of a Savage*, pp. 90–3).
39 *La Revue Blanche*, 1897, pp. 83–4.
40 Louvre MS, pp. 52–3, 89–92.
41 Segalen, *Lettres*, 1950, pp. 118–120.
42 ibid, p. 122.
43 Malingue, *Letters*, 1948, p. 212.

44 Louvre MS, pp. 177, 179, 181, 183.
45 Compare also Louvre MS, p. 179 and *Femmes et Cheval Blanc*, 1903 (W636).
46 Segalen, *Lettres*, 1950, p. 188.
47 Loize, 1966, p. 85.
48 Malingue, *Letters*, 1948, pp. 214–15.
49 Loize, 1966, p. 85.
50 *La Revue Blanche*, 1897, pp. 177–83.
51 Malingue, *Letters*, 1948, p. 219.
52 See pp. 144–5.
53 Louvre MS, pp. 205–346.
54 1903. Facsimile published 1918 (trans. *Intimate Journals of Paul Gauguin*, 1923).
55 Segalen, *Lettres*, 1950, pp. 217–18.
56 Malingue, *Letters*, 1948, pp. 225–6.
57 Segalen, *Lettres*, 1950, p. 186.
58 ibid, p. 227.
59 Louvre MS, pp. 3–25.
60 Loize, 1966, p. 157.
61 Segalen, *Lettres*, 1950, p. 116.
62 Loize, 1966, pp. 92–5.
63 Cabinet des Dessins, RF7259. (See Huyghe 1951, p. 6, n. 3.)
64 *Les Marges*, Paris, May 1910, pp. 169–74.
65 Rotonchamp, 1906.
66 A complete edition of Gauguin's correspondence is in preparation by Mme Merete Bodelsen.
67 See Huyghe, 1951, pp. 8–9, 15, 33 n.3; Loize/ Griffin, 1961, p. 69; Loize, 1966, pp. 80–8, 126 n.
68 Morice, 1919, p. 174. (See also our p. 105.)

II   The collaboration with Morice

60   Above left: Self-portrait caricature, after the 1888 painting *Les Misérables*. Pen and ink. Letter to Emile Schuffenecker, October 8th, 1888

61   Above right: Charles Morice. *c*.1890. Drawing by Baud Bovy

The axis between Gauguin and Morice fostered and has continued to foster as much partisan bias of opinion as that between Gauguin and his wife. Within the covers of one book published as recently as 1978, we find one author describing Morice as 'that evil-doer of the written word' and another suggesting that 'he has been harshly and unjustly sentenced by Gauguin infatuates'.[1]

For Morice the sad outcome has been that a young poet, favoured disciple of Mallarmé, who in 1889 had published a critique of contemporary literature in France[2] that was much acclaimed in Symbolist circles, is now remembered as little more than the intrusive ghost-writing partner in Gauguin's *Noa Noa*. Only in two editions (1897 and 1901) did Morice's name appear alongside Gauguin's as author. Furthermore, he spent much of his life after Gauguin's death publishing letters, articles, reviews and a monograph on the painter.

Within months of publication of the 1901 *La Plume* edition de Monfried was reporting to Gauguin that 'everyone thinks that your book is tarnished by the collaboration with Charles Morice, whose poems are trivial. I haven't read it myself, so

I can't give you a personal opinion.'[3] 'It can't really do me any harm', Gauguin shrewdly observes in his reply.[4]

This hero-and-villain tradition begs questions about how and why the collaboration evolved and survived and, in the light of those, questions about the grounds for all the criticism – moral and ethical as well as literary – that has been heaped upon Morice's participation.

Gauguin first met Morice in 1890. Morice, younger by twelve years, was an ardent admirer of Gauguin's art, perhaps inspired by Mallarmé. He was one of forty-five guests at Gauguin's farewell banquet in 1891 and before he left, Gauguin thought well enough of Morice not only to lend him 500 francs, but also to entrust him with management of his outstanding financial affairs in Paris. This gave rise to a catalogue of complaints in Gauguin's letters over the next two years. 'Every month I have been expecting money from Morice with whom I left it, plus the proceeds . . . neither money nor news' (March 1892);[5] 'As for Morice, I am resigned to the loss of money that he has of mine and am astonished at his silence and his behaviour' (August 1892);[6] 'I have received five lines from Morice who . . . alleges that he has written me many letters and sent me money. Lies!' (November 1892);[7] 'This means that Morice has pinched 1353 francs from me which would have saved my life . . . I have to admit that this theft dumbfounds me, for theft it is';[8] 'On my return I shall go into the matter at first hand. If I can get hold of the money I left there I shall have 1300 francs' (April 1893).[9]

Just how the matter was resolved when he got home we do not know. There are fewer letters in Paris of course, because most of his correspondents were there. The major exception was his wife in Copenhagen, but Gauguin never went out of his way to discuss the credit side of his finances with her. We do know that Gauguin's immediate financial embarrassment was alleviated by a legacy of nearly 10,000 francs from the estate of his uncle who had died in Orléans. We also know that he was very preoccupied with other things. Possibly these factors took some of the heat out of the matter. At all events, Gauguin's friendship with Morice was rapidly revived. Within two or three months of Gauguin's return, Morice had written a preface for the catalogue of Gauguin's exhibition at Durand-Ruel's gallery (November–December 1893) and they had initiated the collaboration on Noa Noa.

The very idea of a collaboration may seem at odds with Gauguin's ferociously independent spirit. But there had been other partnership attempts – with Laval in Martinique for instance, with Van Gogh in Arles. When Gauguin planned each of the Tahiti trips he intended to go with others rather than alone and more than once he regretted that there was no one with him – to discuss art among other things.[10] It may also be worth noting that each partnership attempt was characterized by failure and that in a letter of 1899 he reflected that 'reading puts me in touch with others without mingling with the crowd, of which I have always been afraid.'[11]

In the case of the partnership with Morice there was a practical side to the arrangement. The initial momentum behind Noa Noa was to foster a greater public understanding of Gauguin's painting in Paris. Gauguin wanted to get the project off the ground as quickly as possible and it is typical both of his impatience and of his practical urgency that he should enlist whatever help was needed. He was not a writer himself; Morice was a professional and one who, in theory at least, knew the publishing industry better than a painter would. If it transpired that Gauguin made a bad choice on several counts, he did nevertheless make it. If he should have known better already than to trust Morice, there were also good reasons why he should have chosen him. Gauguin was consistently attracted to younger men intellectually more articulate than himself (Bernard, Sérusier – again relationships not always crowned with success). He had written of poets as 'the necessary intermediary not only between humanity and nature, but also between man and thought'[12] and shared many ideas with Morice. Morice had written on Verlaine[13] and was close to Mallarmé, both of whom Gauguin admired. The main drift of Morice's *Littérature de Tout à l'Heure* had been the advocacy of elusiveness in poetry, of a language of suggestion and correspondences, of thoughts that were veiled rather than explicit – all of them Symbolist principles close to the heart of Gauguin's painting and writing.[14]

Morice retrospectively explained the early years of the collaboration like this:

It was studying works exhibited in the rue Lafitte in 1893[15] that the idea came to me of a literary composition on the themes of the painter, in which he would work side-by-side with a poet. The plan emerged: a section of narration which would be Gauguin's and a section of poems which would be mine.

Gauguin agreed to my proposal enthusiastically. He quickly drafted the notes from which I wrote the chapters wherein *'le conteur parle'* [the story-teller speaks]. My own work, more delicate, took longer. I did not wait to finish my section before I submitted to Gauguin my rendering of the narrative chapters, and these he approved: this version is the only true first draft.[16]

Apart from the intractable problem of who first had the idea of *Noa Noa*, this is all very plausible. Later events tend to support the possibility that Morice made the first move and urged Gauguin to proceed with the idea: he had at least as much to gain from it. He successively tells Gauguin of his plans for a published dialogue between them embodying an 'aesthetic autobiography'; for a *'pantomime lyrique (ballet doré)'* based on *Noa Noa*; for a sequel to *Noa Noa*; for an exhibition he would organize; for a public donation to the state, and so on.[17] By 1901 Gauguin had seen it all before and replied with a resigned shrug: 'Isn't this just another of your usual drummed-up enthusiasms, doomed to end in disappointment?'[18] But in a very different frame of mind, freshly back in Paris in 1893, Gauguin may well have reacted as enthusiastically as Morice describes.

In 1910, stung by a reference to *Noa Noa* as a marvellous book by Paul Gauguin, Morice became more forthright about the partnership.

Noa Noa is mine, my dear Montfort, far more than Gauguin's. I collaborated with him as a poet or an artist collaborates with nature. I studied his paintings in depth and we discussed it intimately and then I wrote it. Not only did the painter not compose a single one of the prose poems and verses that make up half of the book, but even the chapters of straight biography comprise a labour of transposition in which the relatives roles of the raw material [*confiances*] and those parts which are realization would be difficult to disentangle. Of course this book could not have existed without Gauguin . . . but is this any reason for you to omit my name alongside his?[19]

Again everything he says here is beyond dispute and it is difficult not to sympathize with him. The notes, amendments and additions that Gauguin made to the Draft MS give every appearance of a fragmentary document that is under discussion and the narrative stories that appear in the Louvre MS but were not part of the Draft MS must have been a part of those discussions.[20] The transition from the Draft MS to the Louvre MS is very much as Morice describes. Gauguin's narratives are edited and refined; Morice's writing uses Gauguin's imagery as its motif.

The clearest statement by Gauguin about *Noa Noa* tells us little more. 'Before leaving', he told a journalist in 1895, 'I shall publish in collaboration with my friend

Ia Orana Gauguin .1.

La princesse entrait dans ma chambre et j'étais sur mon lit, souffrant, vêtu ~~Xar~~ seulement d'un simple pareo - Quelle tenue pour recevoir une femme de qualité.

‟ Tu es malade, me dit-elle, je viens te voir „.

Et tu te nommes lui dis-je .. Vaïtua.

Vaïtua était une vraie princesse, si toutefois il en existe depuis que les Européens ont dans ce pays rabaissé tout à leur niveau. Le fait est qu'elle arrivait là en simple mortelle - Pieds nus, une fleur odorante à l'oreille, une robe noire. (Elle était en deuil de son oncle le roi Pomaré qui venait de mourir). Son père à elle, Tamatoa, malgré le frottement Européen, les réceptions d'amiral, n'avait jamais voulu être autre chose qu'un royal Maorie, gigantesque batteur d'hommes dans ses moments de colère,

62 Opening page of Gauguin's MS for the story of Princess Vaïtua. First published by Morice, 1920 (see pp. 48–9)

Table Des Matières

63 Contents page of the Louvre MS, 1894/5

Charles Morice a book about my life in Tahiti and my views on art. Morice comments in verse on the works that I have brought back with me. In short the book will be a statement about why and how I made the journey.'[21]

When *Noa Noa* had failed to materialize by the time Gauguin prepared for his second departure to Tahiti in May 1895, he again had his hands full with many other problems. It was still in his interest to leave *Noa Noa* in someone else's hands. Apart from his waning patience and his decision to give Molard final power of attorney over publishing matters, there is no reason to believe that at this stage Gauguin was anything but satisfied with Morice's literary collaboration. He had after all laboriously copied out the joint text as it stood in 1894/5 and had left his original draft material in Morice's care.

So in what way was Morice culpable? That he was not the most prompt repayer of debts seems fairly clear and de Monfried mentioned to Gauguin at one point that he was advising Vollard to deal with someone 'more responsible and solvent' than Morice.[22] He failed to get the book published until too late and he did not keep Gauguin informed. In most other respects he did all that was expected of him, only too slowly.

Inasmuch as Gauguin retained interest in the project, it is not really clear whether or not he had second thoughts about the collaboration. His suggestions (to Mme Morice?) about publishing the poetry separately from his text might imply a change of mind. However, when de Monfried mentioned the common opinion that Noa Noa was 'tarnished' by Morice's poetry, Gauguin's reply is significant.

> What you say about the contribution of Morice to Noa Noa doesn't displease me. For me the collaboration had two objectives. It wasn't like other collaborations – that is to say two authors working in harness. It occurred to me that I could bring out the character of 'savages' more clearly by comparing it to our own. It seemed an original idea for me to write with a primitive simplicity, side-by-side with the style of a cultured man – Morice. So I conceived and directed the collaboration with this intention. What is more, not being a professional writer myself, I thought it might tell us a little about the relative value of the two – the naïve clumsy savage or the corrupted [pourri] product of civilization.[23]

The theme of the savage/cultured contrast will be returned to in connection with Noa Noa's purpose, but it should be understood at this point that the last sentence does not imply any personal vindictiveness towards Morice. The rottenness of all things European (including himself) is an obsessive theme of Gauguin's writing. He talks for instance of 'this filthy Europe' and of 'the putrid kiss of the Ecole des Beaux Arts'.

When Gauguin's letters to de Monfried were first published in 1918, they aggravated the established anti-Morice tradition to such an extent that Morice was obliged to add a note to his monograph, to be published the following year. (At this point Morice had not seen anything of the Louvre MS except the excerpts published in Les Marges, 1910; he did not know how if at all it was changed since 1894/5.) 'In order never to have to return to the subject', Morice first gave the resumé of Noa Noa's genesis that we have already quoted above.[24] He then continued:

> If later on, in his solitude in Tahiti or Dominique, Gauguin rewrote Noa Noa in his own hand and introduced some alterations to the original edition according to his own taste; if he said that he had 'conceived and directed the collaboration' in order to show the superiority of the naïve and brutal savage over the 'corrupted civilized man' – all of these things are quite beside the point . . .

> But I cannot let it be said that I have modified Gauguin's text without his consent: if the truth is to be told, there never was a Gauguin text. All of the pages of Noa Noa had been read in manuscript and approved by him.[25]

The phrase 'if the truth is to be told, there never was a Gauguin text' has been interpreted in the past as Morice's denial of the existence of the Draft MS, which he had sold eleven years earlier.[26] This does not stand close examination since earlier in the same note Morice says quite clearly that 'Gauguin quickly drafted the notes from which I worked',[27] i.e. the Draft MS. Even so, the reference must have caused some comment at the time since a year later, in the second edition of his monograph, the offending phrase is deftly excised.[28]

We know from the Louvre MS that Gauguin approved the first phase of Morice's writing and editing. What he had no chance to approve was first the new material that Morice completed later and secondly the continual editorial refinement to which Morice subjected Gauguin's text. Some of these alterations were trivial but obsessive rewordings – 'more than once' for 'several times' and so on. Others exhibit moral caution. For instance when the story of Vaïtua appeared in *La Revue Blanche* in 1897, there were characteristic modifications from the Louvre MS.[29] When the princess lies drinking and smoking on Gauguin's creaking bed, her naked feet no longer caress the wooden bedpost 'like the tongue of a tiger around a skull', but instead 'with an involuntary mechanical gesture, continuously'. Furthermore, in the revised version she no longer says, on her way out: 'I think I have drunk plenty of absinthe. I am leaving. I shall do something stupid'.[30]

The intended contrast between the painter's simple narrative and the poet's elaborate interpretations is very clear in the early stages of *Noa Noa*. Compare any of Gauguin's crisp descriptions of walking through the Tahitian landscape in the Draft MS with the following passage from Morice's opening chapter *'Songeries'* (Dreams) in the Louvre MS.

> The charm, the majesty, the luxuriance, the intoxication of the *Forest* welcomes, lures, entwines in its fatal, overpowering embrace the pilgrim on his way to the Arorai, the mountain which touches the sky. Noa Noa! No animal life. Total silence. But what violent harmonies among the perfumes of nature which bemuse the travelling artist! What great beauty in the multi-coloured explosion of leaves, fruits, blossoms! His eyes – still transfixed by the endless physical splendours to be witnessed at night and by daylight's feast of sensual delights, so chaste and naïve – probe among the celebration of nature, searching out that all-conquering feminine beauty, the soul of the *Forest*.[31]

The passage is typical in being based on Gauguin's written and visual imagery and yet wholly distinct from anything that Gauguin himself could write. This, it seems, was Gauguin's highly original intention. However, the cumulative effect of Morice's editorial interventions was – by the 1901 version – so to reduce the contrast, that the effect is largely gone. To this extent he did *Noa Noa* a disservice, by his apparent inability to leave it alone.

Reading Morice's prose now, we are tempted to think that Gauguin may have approved this heavily embroidered language, almost tongue in cheek, for its corruptness. But perhaps we would be projecting too much of our sensibilities upon the taste and manners of 1890's Paris. If Gauguin thought at all along those lines, then it was only retrospectively, after a long absence from Paris. In 1903 he writes, 'One could not believe how in the primitive life, one's opinions change. . . Nothing troubles my judgement [now], not even the judgement of others. . . . I and I alone choose, without any constraint, without even a pair of gloves.'[32]

Gauguin's attitude towards Morice fluctuated, but there is little doubt that he used Morice to his own advantage whenever possible.

Today we find Morice's lace-ruffed style so unsympathetic and so incompatible with Gauguin's natural manner that our instinct is not to consider it very seriously. Maybe, finally, this approximates to what Gauguin hoped for from his readers.

Notes

1 Guérin and Andersen, *Writings of a Savage*, 1978, pp. xxxix, xiii, respectively.
2 *La Littérature de Tout à l'Heure*, Paris, 1889.
3 Segalen, *Lettres*, 1950, p. 227.
4 ibid, p. 188.
5 Malingue, *Letters*, 1948, p. 166.
6 ibid, p. 174.
7 ibid, p. 176.
8 Segalen, *Lettres*, 1950, p. 65.
9 Malingue, *Letters*, 1948, p. 181.
10 ibid, p. 180.
11 ibid, p. 221.
12 *Notes Synthétiques* (see bibliography) n.p.
13 *Verlaine, An Analysis . . .*, Paris, 1888.
14 e.g. Morice, 1889, pp. 377–84.
15 Gauguin's exhibition at Durand–Ruel.
16 Morice, 1919, pp. 173–4 n.
17 Segalen, *Lettres*, 1950, pp. 207–17.
18 Malingue, *Letters*, 1948, p. 226.
19 Loize, 1966, pp. 97–8.
20 See p. 48.
21 *Écho de Paris*, May 13th, 1895.
22 Segalen, *Lettres*, 1950, p. 215.
23 ibid, p. 227.
24 See p. 102.
25 Morice, 1919, pp. 173–4 n.
26 Loize, 1966, p. 100.
27 Morice, 1919, p. 173 n. See also our p. 102.
28 Morice, 1920, p. 188 n.
29 See pp. 49–52.
30 See Louvre MS, pp. 38–9, and *La Revue Blanche*, 1897, pp. 84–5.
31 Louvre MS, p. 15.
32 *Avant et Après*, p. 78 (*Intimate Journal*, p. 141).

III Maori mythology: Tehamana and Moerenhout

64 *Mahana Atua* (Feast or Day of the gods). *c.*1894/5. Woodcut, 35 × 20.5 cm. Guérin 42. National Gallery of Art, Washington

In his chapter *'Songeries'*, Morice wrote, 'Here then is Tahiti, *faithfully imagined'*,[1] a paradox that brings us close to the second reason for confused difference of opinion over *Noa Noa*, namely the originality and authenticity of Gauguin's material.

It is well enough known that the Tahiti Gauguin had read about in Paris – an island paradise untouched by Western civilization – no longer existed and that his disillusionment with the effects upon Tahitian life of colonial rule and missionary education was almost immediate. There was virtually no indigenous art, no idols; traditional religious ritual had virtually disappeared, the ancient burial grounds and temples were in ruins. Although some ageing chiefs might still be able and willing to recite songs and legends for the benefit of Westerners, the oral traditions that had kept Maori mythology alive were gone.[2] Anyway, according to one researcher, the Polynesian sense of humour cast serious doubt on the few native sources that there were: 'In order to see what a Maori can do in the way of gulling Europeans, and in inducing them to accept absurd statements, one has but to peruse that amazing collection of rubbish, *Maori Symbolism*.'[3] No surprise then that we find Gauguin writing early in the Draft MS: '. . . shall I manage to rediscover traces of that distant past . . . to rediscover the ancient hearth and rekindle the fire amidst all these ashes? And all this totally alone, with no support?'

In fact and by good chance Gauguin had stumbled upon the most respectable European source, J. A. Moerenhout's two-volume *Voyages aux Îles du Grand Océan* (1837). Moerenhout, a Belgian, had worked in Polynesia in the 1820s and '30s as consul successively for the American and French governments. His book is a comprehensive attempt to describe the geography, life, culture, mythology, religion of the Pacific Islands.

That Gauguin used Moerenhout's book so extensively and wove his material into the fabric of *Noa Noa* has been treated variously as plagiarism and fraud. Loize tries to 'absolve' Gauguin by passing blame for most of the borrowing and its attendant shame onto Morice.[4] If 'shame' seems a strong word, read another biographer: 'One can understand Gauguin's need to hide from his European fellows the humiliation that his knowledge of Maori religion came from a book – worse yet, a book written by a Belgian, published in Paris, and available in the Bibliothèque Nationale.'[5]

Gauguin was lent a copy of the book by a French colonial called Goupil in Papeete, probably in the spring of 1892.[6] (A suggestion that he already had access to the book in Paris is not convincing.)[7] Gauguin enthused about his discovery in a letter to Sérusier: 'What a religion the ancient religion of Oceania! What a marvel . . .',[8] and to his wife: 'I am fairly pleased with my last works and feel there is dawning in me an Oceanic character.'[9] To de Monfried he mentions 'documents which are building up'.[10] In other letters he talks of 'studies' that he is accumulating, and the formative influence of Moerenhout's book upon the subject matter of his painting was considerable.[11] *Manao Tupapau*, an imaginative painting of a Maori girl enveloped in thoughts and fears of the spirits of the dead, is an important example (Plate 16).

The documents and studies of which Gauguin speaks are probably references to the material contained in his notebook *Ancien Culte Mahorie*. The text of this small album, beautifully illustrated with Gauguin's original watercolours, is all taken from Moerenhout, mostly from the chapters on '*Religion*' and '*Culte*' in Volume I.[12] Apart from spelling mistakes, the copying is usually verbatim, including many of Moerenhout's asides, although Gauguin became more discriminating as he worked through the book. Some gods in Moerenhout's lists are omitted altogether and some narratives – the story of Hiro for example[13] – are stripped to essentials.

Gauguin brought the notebook back with him to Paris. In his Draft MS he uses some of the material – the story of Rouahatou, a prayer, an old Maori saying and the legend of Roua – and makes notes of other legends to be developed. The section on Roua and the birth of the stars was pasted onto page 20 of the Draft MS on a separate sheet of paper. Possibly the idea of incorporating material from the *Ancien Culte Mahorie* emerged from discussion between Gauguin and Morice?

In the Louvre MS, this hesitant beginning is developed into a very long chapter – Chapter VIII, '*La Génèse Polynésienne*' — which, apart from a short interlude of narrative, is quoted directly from *Ancien Culte Mahorie*.[14] We must assume that this work was undertaken by Morice with Gauguin's full knowledge and approval if not active collaboration. The copying is fairly accurate (preserving Gauguin's mistakes), apart from one or two examples of editing which are odd rather than careless. To follow one transcription right through: where Moerenhout describes the patron gods 'of dramatic artists, singers, choreographers', it becomes for Gauguin: 'of artists, singers, actors and choreographers' and finally for Morice: 'of singers, comedians and dancers'.[15] In another example, where Gauguin follows Moerenhout in writing: 'In the society of the Aréois, prostitution was a principle and infanticide an obligation', Morice writes: 'In the society of the Aréois, prostitution was a sacred obligation.'[16]

The subsequent dispute over Gauguin's borrowing from Moerenhout arose because from the start Gauguin implies that Tehamana, his thirteen-year-old *vahine*, taught him all that he knew about Maori lore. In the Draft MS he writes: 'Conversations about what happens in Europe, about God, about the Gods. She learns from me, I learn from her . . .' When, soon afterwards, he introduces Moerenhout's legends of the stars with the words, 'She, in turn, tells me the names of the stars in her language', the implication is fairly clear.[17] In the Louvre MS there can no longer be any doubt of the intention. An

65 Below left: Hina and Tefatou. *c*.1892. Pen and watercolour, 12.5 × 12 cm. Ancien Culte Mahorie MS, p. 7

66 Below right: Ornament from a Marquesan oar. Carved wood. British Museum (Museum of Mankind), London

67 Opposite: Idol with a Shell. 1893. Ironwood, mother of pearl, bone. h. 27 cm. Gray 99. Private collection, France

extended version of this introduction runs as follows: 'At night in bed we had long discussions, long and often serious. I searched in the soul of this child for traces of a distant past . . . she knew by heart the names of all the gods of the Maori Olympus. She knew their history, how they created the world . . . I have no idea how she reconciled Taaroa and Jesus in her beliefs. I think she venerated them both . . . she gave me a complete course in Tahitian theology.'[18] The style is Morice's, but it would be a nonsense to suggest that Gauguin did not approve – if not indeed contrive – the shameless fiction. (There would have been no conflict in Tehamana's mind, of course, between Christian and Maori faiths, because she would have known nothing at all of the Maori Olympus or of Tahitian mythology.)

Conversely, other aspects of the Louvre MS *expose* this same fiction. Not only were several footnotes added later (in Gauguin's hand) saying 'taken from Morenhout',[19] but there are references to Moerenhout – direct and indirect – actually in the written

68 Above left: Detail from *Human Anguish*. 1888. W304. Ordrupgaard Coll., Copenhagen

69 Above right: Detail from *Breton Eve*. 1889. Pastel and watercolour, 34.6 × 31 cm. W333. Marion Koogler McNay Art Institute, San Antonio, Texas

text. These include: 'When Tehura had told me all she knew on this subject, I found out all I could about it'; or 'I complete the lesson from Tehura with the help of documents found in the memoir of the former consul, Morenhout [sic]. I am obliged to M. Goupil, settler in Tahiti, for access to this publication', or – most charming of all – 'Who created the sky and the earth? Morenhout and Tehura answered me . . .'!.[20] What more open declaration of the wedding of fact and fiction could one expect?

The issue has only been contentious because concepts of originality and of 'truth' have been applied to Gauguin which are quite alien to his thinking. Gauguin was not inhibited by conventions of originality – one reason why he aroused the anger of his peers. (Cézanne was furious at his stylistic borrowings and, as Pissarro said, 'he is always poaching . . . now he is pillaging the savages'.[21]) Borrowing ready-made material was not for Gauguin something that biographers need defend him against; he

70 Above left: Detail from *Where do we come from?* . . . 1897 (see Plate 81)

71 Above right: Detail from *Soyez Amoureuses Vous Serez Heureuses*. 1898/9. Woodcut. Guérin 58

was not party to moralistic obsessions with originality. If a motif was available and of value to him, then it was only natural to use it. Coincidentally, he later defended Pissarro on the same issue. 'He has looked at everyone's work you say! Well why not? Everyone has looked at him too but denies him. He was one of my masters but I don't disown him.'[22]

The low store that he put on originality *per se* may be seen as well in his repeated use of his own images. The same practice pervades his writing: re-use of phrases, structures, images. His *Cahier pour Aline* begins, after the dedication, 'scattered notes, without sequence as in dreams, as in life, all made of fragments'. The words reappear verbatim seven years later in *Avant et Après*.[23]

The issue of 'truth' is no more relevant than that of originality. *Noa Noa* was never presented as a purely factual account. Gauguin dealt in fictions. In *Diverses Choses* he wrote a long section on the falseness of truth and the truthfulness of falsehood,[24] and again we may find confirmation from the character of his painting, in its weaving between external reality and internal fantasy. There is nothing he castigates more in art than 'this stupid precision which binds us to material reality'.[25] Two examples from the Draft MS will demonstrate the elasticity of Gauguin's concepts of truth and reality.

Chapter VI begins with his journey around the island to Taravao. Near the start he mentions: 'Arrive at a small valley. Several people live there and want to go on living in the old way – description of the picture *Matamua/Autrefois* and of *Hina Maruru*.'[26] In the Louvre MS this invented valley – born of what he would have wanted to see – is described in more detail:

> . . . a little valley whose inhabitants still live in the ancient Maori fashion. They are happy and calm. They dream, they love, they sleep, they sing – they pray and I see distinctly, even though they are not there, the statues of their female deities. Statues of Hina and festivals in honour of the Goddess of the Moon. The idol is of one single block, 10 feet from shoulder to shoulder and 40 feet high. On its head it bore, in the form of a bonnet, an enormous reddish stone. They were dancing around the idol according to ancient rites.[27]

The description would appear to be based upon the painting *Hina Maruru* and includes a frank confession that the statues did not exist. However, the image of the idol is not purely imaginative. Gauguin's description of it is taken word for word from an account of the colossal Easter Island statues in Volume II of Moerenhout.[28] Clearly it was reading this passage that inspired the painting in the first place.

If the drafting of the passage above was Morice's work, the spirit and the method are entirely in keeping with autograph Gauguin. The story of *Pape Moë* which appears in the previous chapter of the Draft MS[29] and as the subject of a painting and a carving is a relevant authentic example. The story's central thread was Gauguin's journey through a part of the interior of Tahiti. This was a real journey and the main incident in the story may or may not relate to a particular real incident. But it is so interwoven with other types of source material – not just the photograph that we know he followed so closely (Plates 14, 73, 74), but also separate Polynesian legends describing respectively a princess diving through a 'hole' in a river into the underworld, and a royal eel who was King of Lake Vaihiria[30] – that we can no longer talk in terms of perceived reality as a simple source. It is closer to the truth to think of Gauguin perceiving reality through the filter of his educated imagination, and vice versa. This makes sense of Gauguin's own description of the painting *Vahine no te Tiare* as 'what my eyes *veiled by my heart* perceived'[31] and of Morice's phrase 'faithfully imagined'. What Gauguin painted and wrote about was mostly not in front of his eyes. The American John Lafarge, in Tahiti in 1890, wrote in a similar vein: 'the absence of any outer form to antiquity makes me seek it all the more in the nature which surrounds me, in the imaginary presence of the people who lived within it.'[32]

The instincts and the techniques that characterize Gauguin's use in *Noa Noa* of material from Moerenhout are quite compatible with Gauguin's work as a whole. He spoke of a literary part and a musical part in his painting. The ready-made mythology that he lifted from Moerenhout was highly charged literary material. The device of Tehamana/Tehura as a mouthpiece was a musical or poetic means of reconciling it to

72 *Matamua/Autrefois* (Times gone by). s. & d. 1892. 93 × 72 cm. W467. Coll. Baron Thyssen-Bornemisza. (See p. 33)

73 Above: Tahitian girl drinking from a spring. Photograph, *c.*1880s

74 Opposite: *Pape Moë* (Mysterious water). *c.*1893/5. Oak, partly painted, 81.5 × 62 cm. Gray 107. Present whereabouts unknown

75 Top: Illustration to the legend of creation. *c.*1892. Pen and watercolour, 10.5 × 17 cm. Ancien Culte Mahorie MS, p. 12

76 Prow ornament from a Marquesan canoe. Carved wood. Private collection

the semi-factual content of the narrative. For a biographer to write that 'a far worse fault in *Noa Noa* is that Gauguin as author is only a little more realistic and objective than Gauguin the painter'[33] is somewhat beside the point. More relevant perhaps is the speculation by other authors that further incidents in Gauguin's account of himself – his relationship with the renowned Titi, for instance; his intimacy with Princess Vaïtua; his single-handed fight with fifteen fishermen; or even his suicide – may also be more fiction than fact.[34]

Notes

1 Louvre MS, p. 11.
2 Lafarge, 1914, pp. 333–4; Bovis, 1855, pp. 65–6.
3 Best, 1942, p. 187.
4 Loize, 1966, pp. 74–5.
5 Andersen, *Writings of a Savage*, p. xv.
6 Louvre MS, p. 131; Field, 1977, p. 75.
7 Gray, 1963, p. 49.
8 *Writings of a Savage*, p. 59.
9 Malingue, *Letters*, 1948, p. 170.
10 Segalen, *Lettres*, 1950, p. 54.
11 Field, 1977, Ch. III.
12 Moerenhout, 1837, Vol. I, pp. 419–574; Vol. II, pp. 25, 81–3, 205–11, 269–70.
13 *Ancien Culte Mahorie*, p. 17; Moerenhout, Vol. I, p. 447. See Pl. 59.
14 Louvre MS, pp. 129 ff.
15 Moerenhout, Vol. I, p. 451; *Ancien Culte Mahorie*, p. 18; Louvre MS, p. 144.
16 Moerenhout, Vol. I, p. 495; *Ancien Culte Mahorie*, p. 31; Louvre MS, p. 163.
17 p. 37.
18 Louvre MS, pp. 129–30.
19 ibid, e.g. pp. 130, 153, 199. (He always misspells Moerenhout.)
20 ibid, pp. 151, 131, 134. (For the spelling of 'Tehemana' as 'Tehura', see Note 55, p. 77.)
21 Pissarro, *Letters to Lucien*, 1943, p. 221.
22 *Racontars de Rapin*, p. 35.
23 *Avant et Après*, p. 16.
24 *Writings of a Savage*, pp. 144 ff.
25 (of the painter Bouguereau). Segalen, *Lettres*, 1950, p. 121.
26 p. 33. See also Note 53, p. 77.
27 Louvre MS, pp. 98–9.
28 Moerenhout, Vol. II, pp. 269–70; *Ancien Culte Mahorie*, p. 51.
29 p. 32.
30 Gray, 1963, p. 63.
31 p. 20.
32 Lafarge, 1914, p. 333.
33 Danielsson, 1966, p. 168.
34 See Andersen, for instance, in *Writings of a Savage* and in *Gauguin's Paradise Lost*, 1971.

IV   The purpose of Noa Noa: the primitive and the civilized

When Gauguin first mentioned *Noa Noa*, in a letter to his wife, he described its purpose: 'to facilitate understanding of my paintings'.[1] He had invested two hard and lonely years in these paintings and the reception accorded them at his 1893 exhibition had disappointed him. His description of the show as an outstanding success is another reminder that reality for Gauguin could exist in the mind independently of external fact. 'Don't these people understand anything?' he burst out later in *Diverses Choses*. 'Is it too ingenuous for overly witty refined Parisians?'[2]

There is other evidence that his Tahitian paintings required explanation. The critic Mauclair had written that 'the coarseness and brutality of his work is revolting'.[3] The Director of the Beaux Arts had told him: 'I do not feel able to encourage your art. It revolts me and I do not understand it.'[4] A critic at the 1893 exhibition saw his paintings as 'the fantasies of a poor cracked mind . . . the worst sort of outrage against art, against nature'.[5] Strindberg wrote to him: 'I cannot understand your art and cannot like it. I have no grasp of your art, which is now exclusively Tahitian.'[6] Later on, the sympathetic critic Fontainas was to repeat Strindberg's detrimental comparison of Gauguin with Puvis de Chavannes, suggesting that Gauguin was unable to make his ideas understood.[7]

Gauguin had serious reservations about writings on art and it has been observed more than once that when he did attempt detailed written explanation of a painting he was not at his most convincing.[8] He wrote to Fontainas, quite sincerely: 'I have preserved silence and shall continue to do so, being persuaded that truth does not emerge from argument but from the work that is done.'[9] He shared Mallarmé's view of the critic as 'a gentleman who meddles with what doesn't concern him' and generally professed himself against intellectual activity, first because it was debilitating to the artist and secondly because it confused rather than clarified one's understanding of art. In a fictitious conversation with a critic in *Diverses Choses*, Gauguin is asked 'why don't you explain Symbolism to me?' He answers: 'How nice it would be if you spoke to me in Hebrew, a language which neither you nor I understand. That would make the situation analogous . . . my paintings probably speak Hebrew, which you do not understand, so there is no point continuing this conversation.'[10] 'Take care not to step on the foot of a learned idiot', he warns in *Avant et Après*, 'His bite is incurable.'[11]

As all of this might suggest, it was natural that Gauguin should want to 'explain' or complement his paintings in a manner that was oblique. Morice's preface to the *Revue Blanche* excerpts in 1897, which says, 'What you will find here is not art criticism, but narrations – and other things besides',[12] would have met with Gauguin's approval.

So the initial, urgent purpose of *Noa Noa* was explanation. Gauguin's early expectation was that something would appear soon enough after his 1893 exhibition to be seen in its context. As the work took shape, so did the nature of the explanation. The narration and the mythology would unfold the experience behind the paintings; some

77 *Self-portrait with Idol. c.*1891. 46 × 33 cm. W415. Marion Koogler McNay Art Institute, San Antonio, Texas

78 Above left: *Oviri. c.*1894. Woodcut, coloured with watercolour, 21 × 12 cm. Guérin 48. Louvre MS, p. 61

79 Above right: *Oviri. c.*1894/5. Stoneware, partly glazed, h. 74 cm. Gray 113.
Private collection, Paris

paintings would be described; Morice's original verse and prose would form an imaginative response to the painted images. With the clarification of these means, the second purpose of the book also became clear – to contrast the quality of life and thought of the civilized European with that of the primitive or 'savage'. On the face of it, this contrast was to be achieved by the counterposing of his own instinct and style with that of a cultured European, Morice.

In this contrast Gauguin cast himself as the savage; *Noa Noa* may be seen as just a part of a very complete image that he steadily put together of himself in this role. It relates to his coloured memories of childhood in Peru, to his romancing about Inca blood in his veins and to the muffled symbolic resonances that his imagination heard in Brittany as his wooden clogs struck the granite soil. 'There are two sides to my nature,' he wrote to his wife in 1888, 'the Indian and the sensitive. The sensitive has disappeared so that the Indian can move forward with conviction.'[13] To Redon he wrote that 'Gauguin is finished as far as here [Europe] is concerned, and no more will be seen of him',[14] as if he was steadily fortifying his self-image as an alien to Europe. He inscribed

80 *Matamoë* (Foreigners). s. & d. 1892. 115 × 86 cm. W484. Pushkin Museum, Moscow

'*Oviri*' on his self-portrait relief in Paris[15] and later wanted the frightening herma-phroditic ceramic sculpture of Oviri as his gravestone[16] (Plate 79).

The contrast between this image and the floral style of Morice is powerful, but such a contrast is already present throughout Gauguin's writing, his painting and his sculpture and – for all his protestations – within himself. If we are to take as at all meaningful his proposal (to Mme Morice) that the two collaborators' contributions to *Noa Noa* might be published separately, then maybe it suggests that Gauguin, by this time, had acknowledged the primitive/civilized axis to be strong enough in his own work, without Morice's contribution.

It is certainly this axis that underpins all of his mature work as an artist. His single most important painting in Tahiti is probably the great pageant '*Where do we come from? What are we? Where are we going?*', painted in 1897 as his last testament before his suicide. The questions of its title are all posed in the visual form of an opposition. Its extremes are the depressed introversion and self-awareness of the thinking European on the one hand and on the other the unaffected and irresponsible innocence of the primitive being, who lives, loves, sings and sleeps. Typical is Gauguin's explanation to Morice of the two 'sinister figures' in the shadows 'recording near the tree of science their note of anguish caused by this science itself, in comparison with the simple beings in a virgin nature, which might be the human idea of paradise . . .'[17]

In his Draft MS Gauguin had already set up such a contrast as the central theme of *Noa Noa*. From the start there are asides about the Europeanness of Papeete, the indifference of the French and 'the sickness which the Europeans have brought'.[18] His first mistress, Titi, is rejected because she is half-white and already too civilized, too versed in European standards.[19] In the extraordinary story of the wood-cutter – perhaps the most interesting episode in the MS in terms of its frankness – he explains his momentary lust in terms of a disease of Europe: 'I alone carried the burden of an evil thought, a whole civilization had been before me in evil and had educated me.'[20] The same distinction is drawn again when he brings Tehamana home and returns the gendarme's horse at Taravao. Gauguin describes the gendarme's French wife regarding Tehamana as 'decrepitude staring at the new flowering, the virtue of the law was

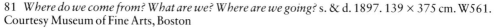

81 *Where do we come from? What are we? Where are we going?* s. & d. 1897. 139 × 375 cm. W561.
Courtesy Museum of Fine Arts, Boston

82 *Te Po* (The night). *c.*1894/5. Woodcut, 20.5 × 35.5 cm. Guérin 15. Nationalmuseum, Stockholm

breathing impurely upon the native but pure unashamedness of trust, faith. And against that so blue sky, I saw with grief this dirty cloud of smoke. I felt ashamed of my race . . .'[21] In the same context, the title of the painting *Matamoë* means 'Strangers'[22] and is usually interpreted as a symbolic image of the self-conscious, alien peacocks in the natural, indigenous landscape. The whole story of the wedding in Chapter VIII is, of course, a parable about European despoliation and native mistrust, and Gauguin's Appendix to *Noa Noa* is subtitled: 'After the work of art – the truth, the dirty truth'.[23]

What is worth noticing, against the grain of the general self-image that Gauguin projects, is that here in *Noa Noa*, a book for Parisians, Gauguin usually sees himself in the role of the guinea-pig European, the 'inferior' civilized man. It is *he* who is intimidated and ashamed, and when he compares the French and Maori characters[24] it is in terms of the transparent openness of his own and the enigmatic nature of Tehamana's.

Other sources too, his letters, his journal, his paintings, suggest that the European Gauguin had by no means ceased to exist. In 1890, when he wrote to Redon in Paris that he was finished as far as that place was concerned, he also said: 'I am taking with me in photographs and drawings a whole little community of comrades who will chat with me every day.'[25] His painting and writing abound in echoes of this collection. What is effectively the title-page of the Louvre *Noa Noa* MS is an image of flowers (Plate 2): it is based directly on a Delacroix still life, of which he had a reproduction.[26] Furthermore, he actually grew French flowers in Tahiti from seeds that de Monfried had sent, and wrote that although the anemones had failed, the irises, dahlias and gladioli had joined with the Tahitian shrubbery to form 'a veritable Eden' around his house.[27]

While in Tahiti his correspondence with friends and others in France (and particularly with Daniel de Monfried) was an all-important life-line. Jénot, the French naval lieutenant who befriended Gauguin on his arrival, recalled that, once he had left the capital, Papeete, 'Gauguin was always joyful at my arrival, because my stay of three or

83 Opposite: p. 239 of the Louvre MS. Two sketches after Delacroix (*Death of Seneca*, upper right, *Arab Encampment*, lower left); a page from Hokusai's *Mangwa* Vol. 5; a facsimile of *Christ bearing the cross*, engraving (1521) by Lucas van Leyden

84 Above: *Te Tiare Farani* (Flowers of France). s. & d. 1891. 72 × 92 cm. W426. Hermitage, Leningrad

four days put him once more in contact with the European, let a shaft of light into his solitude and formed a sort of holiday in his working life . . . he lived an enclosed life as if his mind was sealed in a glass jar.'[28] As far as he could, Gauguin retained contact with Paris. He was an avid reader of the *Mercure de France*, which he received regularly, and later corresponded with its critic, André Fontainas.

In his manuscripts his prodigious abilities are more often than not accredited to Gauguin the Frenchman, rather than to Gauguin the 'savage'. In *Noa Noa*, after his marathon swim in the Grotto of Mara narrative, he turns to Tehamana and says: 'We French, we are never afraid.'[29] During the tunny fishing expedition, he is the Frenchman who brings good luck to the native fishermen.[30] In *Avant et Après* there is a long exposition of his knowledge and experience of the art of fencing[31] and another extraordinary escapade in which he features as the Frenchman who wipes the floor with top American pool players for enormous stakes.[32]

85 *Two women on the beach*. s. & d. 1891. 69 × 91 cm. W434. Louvre (Jeu de Paume), Paris

As Field has so convincingly argued, Gauguin's pictorial language as a whole retained stronger roots in European painting than anything that he subsequently encountered.[33] The painting *Flowers of France* – quite apart from its title – juxtaposes figures and floral still life in a manner that evokes echoes of Redon and, especially, of Degas, whom Gauguin greatly admired. The whole series of two-figure compositions that Gauguin made in Tahiti, images of silent, questioning native women, pursues a mood very close to that of Degas's Parisian images. On reflection, Gauguin's women have a brooding, inturned quality somewhat at odds with descriptions of the lethargic but carefree, loving children of a native paradise. It is true that Gauguin did once describe the natives as sitting immobile for hours gazing sadly at the sky,[34] but the image corresponds far more closely to his concept of the troubled mind of the European. (Field interprets this kind of self-consciousness as an image of intrusive European corruption of the native serenity.[35])

In *Noa Noa*, Gauguin presents us with an image of his conversion from European to 'savage'. The reality around him was of the primitive life in process of being converted by Europeans in the opposite direction. Nevertheless, his determination to realize the conversion shines through the manuscript. At first he appears as the novice: 'Having only just arrived . . . I was in some ways blind', 'coming from Europe I was constantly uncertain . . .' 'Why did I hesitate? . . . Old habits from Europe, probably . . . timidity of expression of our bastardized races'.[36]

As a result of the incident with the beautiful wood-cutter – Chapter IV of the Draft MS – the conversion is completed and celebrated in violent physical aggression and in song. 'Well and truly destroyed indeed, all the old remnant of civilized man in me. I returned at peace, feeling myself thenceforward a different man, a Maori . . . a sweet quietude, a fragrance, a victory and a rejuvenation.'[37]

86 Degas: *Au Café. c.*1877/80. 65.7 × 54.6 cm. Fitzwilliam Museum, Cambridge

87 Above: *Aha oe Feii?* (What, are you jealous?). s. & d. 1892. 68 × 92 cm. W461. Hermitage, Leningrad

88 Opposite: *Nafea Faa Ipoipo?* (When will you marry?). s. & d. 1892. 105 × 77.5 cm. W454. Kunstmuseum, Basel

The nineteenth-century European view of the primitive life contained a strong sense of rejuvenation, of return to the unspoilt infancy of the human race. Gauguin shared this general view, but it also took on a more personal meaning for him: he constantly associated his mature escape from Europe with his own roots, his exotic ancestry, his childhood in Peru and so on. The most potent instance of this was his use of a photograph of his mother for the head of an image of *Exotic Eve* (Plates 94–6) – a very loaded dream image.[38] The notion of rejuvenation lay at the heart of his dream. There is much talk in his letters of the primitive life giving man back his strength; and remember his comment 'two years older, twenty years younger'.[39]

Describing the 1890 population of Papeete, John Lafarge identified 'a few Europeans, who meet the place half way and belong neither to where they came from, nor to the unreality of the place they are in'.[40] Gauguin's prevailing Frenchness was much closer

89 Above: 'Fare'. *c.*1891/3. Pen and ink over pencil, 12 × 8.5 cm. Carnet de Tahiti, p. 101

90 Opposite: Detail from *Te Rerioa* (The Dream). 1897. W557. Courtauld Institute Galleries, London

to this condition than to that of the alien peacocks. He belonged to neither community. The French thought of him as savage[41] and the natives thought of him as French. After recalling his Peruvian ancestry in *Avant et Après*, he acknowledges the duality himself. 'There are many strange mixtures in me. A rough sailor? O.K! But there is race as well – or rather two races', and later, 'You drag your double along with you and yet the two contrive to survive.'[42]

Of course the conversion was impossible. 'Savage' for Gauguin was synonymous

91 Above: *Maruru* (Thanks). *c.*1894/5. Woodcut, trimmed and partly retouched with watercolour. Guérin 23. Based on the 1893 painting *Hina Maruru* (W500). Louvre MS, p. 59. (See p. 33)

92 Opposite top: Guardian spirits of the sea. *c.*1892. Pen and watercolour, 13 × 16 cm. Ancien Culte Mahorie MS, p. 21

93 Opposite bottom: Seated Tahitienne. *c.*1896/7. Watercolour, pen and ink, 19.5 × 17 cm. pasted over p. 172 of the Louvre MS

94 Opposite: *Exotic Eve*. s. & d. 1890. Oil on cardboard, 43 × 25 cm. W389 (lost)

95 Top: Photograph of Gauguin's mother, Aline

96 *Portrait of Gauguin's mother*. *c*.1890. 41 × 33 cm. W389. Staatsgalerie, Stuttgart

97 Above: Night landscape. *c.*1896/7. Watercolour, 23 x 19 cm. Louvre MS, p. 65

98 Opposite: Thatched hut under palm trees. *c.*1896/7. Watercolour, 30 × 22.5 cm. Louvre MS, p. 181

with 'unspoilt' and he had been spoilt by Europe. In one of his last letters to Morice he wrote: 'You were mistaken that day in saying that I was wrong to call myself a savage . . . for there is nothing in my work which astonishes, perplexes, if not this "savage-in-spite-of-myself". That's why my work is inimitable. The work of a man is the explanation of the man.'[43] The 'explanation' of Gauguin to emerge from *Noa Noa* is of a civilized man with a vision of an ideal, primitive existence – a blending of dream and reality, like all of his work. That others recognized the extraordinariness of this fusion is affirmed by de Monfried's advice to him not to consider returning to France at the end of his life: the reality of the dream would have been dispelled, whereas the legend had already afforded him 'the immunity of the great dead'.[44]

Notes

1 Malingue, *Letters*, 1948, p. 187.
2 trans. *Writings of a Savage*, p. 137.
3 Segalen, *Lettres*, 1950, p. 91.
4 *Avant et Après*, p. 181.
5 *(Chronique des Beaux Arts)*. See *Cahier pour Aline*, n.p.
6 *Avant et Après*, p. 19.
7 Malingue, *Letters*, 1948, p. 226.
8 Field, 1977, pp. 113 ff.
9 Malingue, *Letters*, 1948, p. 231.
10 trans. *Writings of a Savage*, p. 131.
11 *Avant et Après*, p. 35.
12 *La Revue Blanche*, 1897, p. 81.
13 Malingue, *Letters*, 1948, p. 94.
14 R. Bacou, *Odilon Redon*, Geneva, 1956, Vol. I, p. 186.
15 Gray, 1963, p. 241.
16 ibid, pp. 64 ff. See Plate 79.
17 Malingue, *Letters*, 1948, p. 227.
18 See Chapter I of Draft MS, pp. 12–16.
19 pp. 14, 16.
20 p. 28.
21 p. 35.
22 Wildenstein, 1958, p. 162.
23 p. 43.
24 p. 35.
25 R. Bacou, op. cit., p. 186.
26 Field, 1977, Pl. 51.
27 Segalen, *Lettres*, 1950, p. 141.
28 Wildenstein, 1958, p. 125.
29 p. 57.
30 p. 40.
31 *Avant et Après*, pp. 131 ff.
32 ibid, p. 29.
33 Field, 1977.
34 Malingue, *Letters*, 1948, p. 163.
35 Field, 1977, pp. 132–6, 223–4.
36 pp. 12–13, 20.
37 p. 28.
38 H. Dorra, 1953.
39 p. 85.
40 Lafarge, 1914, pp. 302–3.
41 O'Brien/Pielkovo, *Letters*, 1923, p. 172.
42 *Avant et Après*, pp. 161, 194.
43 Malingue, *Letters*, 1948, p. 181.
44 Segalen, *Lettres*, 1950, pp. 35–6.

V   Noa Noa: 'Fragrant'

99   *Causeries sans paroles* (Conversations without words). *c.*1900/3? Monotype, 21.5 × 15.5 cm.
Avant et Après MS, p. 155

When Gauguin was asked by a journalist what would be the title of his book, he explained: '*Noa Noa* – a Tahitian word meaning "fragrant". In other words the book will be about what Tahiti exhales.'[1] He repeats this translation with his first mention of '*Noa Noa*' in the Draft MS.[2] The words recur repeatedly in the MS, assuming the character of a thematic chorus – at the end of the wood-cutter story for instance: 'the tree smelt of roses, *Noa Noa*' or, following his union with Tehamana, 'the Tahitian *Noa Noa* pervades the whole of me.'[3] This repetitive device was developed in the Louvre MS where the fragrances of nature form a recurrent theme.

75

au monde qui *m'ait tenu ce langage,* —
ce langage d'enfant, *car il faut l'être,*
n'est-ce pas *pour s'imaginer qu'un*

artiste soit. *quelque chose d'utile ...*

100 Opposite: p. 75 of the Louvre MS. Above: Lovers, watercolour, copy after p. 46 of Ancien Culte Mahorie MS; below: fragment of *Manao Tupapau*, *c.*1894/5. Woodcut, 11.5 × 22.5 cm. Guérin 38

101 Above: *Vairaoumati. c.*1894. Watercolour, pen and ink, 14 × 8 cm. Louvre MS, p. 157

As mentioned earlier the title-page of the Louvre MS bears only a vase of flowers. 'I should like to write as I paint', Gauguin says, 'following my fancy, following the moon, and finding the title long afterwards.'[4] The title of *Noa Noa* and the theme of fragrance appear to have taken shape in this way between 1893 and 1895.

So what should we understand from the perfume of *Noa Noa*? Does it convey a picture of Gauguin's first *Voyage de Tahiti*? Does it explain his paintings? At first reading, *Noa Noa* might appear to conceal the hard facts of his existence there – his poverty, his hunger, his ill-health, the antagonism of the French community and his extreme isolation. We get little sense in the manuscript, except in his Appendix (which anyway was quickly dropped), that within a year of his first arrival in Tahiti he was applying for repatriation,[5] or that his stay was as long as two years largely because he was frustrated in his attempts to return to France. All of this is graphically clear in the bitterness and desperation of his letters. However, if we turn the other way and compare *Noa Noa* with the spectacular and celebratory energy of his paintings, we realize that the book does not paint a naïve paradise image either. *Noa Noa* is a more subtle and complicated account of Gauguin in Tahiti than either the letters or the paintings. The spontaneity of Gauguin's Draft MS offers us a very frank picture of his feelings, of his hesitations and uncertainties as well as his sense of liberation, and throws light on both the confusion and the artifice surrounding his quest for a new identity.

Field describes *Noa Noa* as 'a wish-fulfilment modelled after Pierre Loti'.[6] Loti was the best-selling novelist who had popularized Tahiti in 1880s France with his romance *Rarahu* (1880). Gauguin knew Loti's writing[7] and was of course publicly identified with it, but his strenuous efforts to dissociate himself seem justified. Octave Mirbeau, in an article that was obviously briefed by Gauguin, wrote of Gauguin's work as 'alive with strange beauties whose existence M. Pierre Loti never even suspected'.[8] To Gauguin, Loti was a dilettante European who no more than dipped his toes in the exoticism of Tahiti. Beyond confirming for us the prevalence of a European pre-occupation with the distant primitive life as a picturesque and exotic dream, the comparison between Gauguin and Loti has little to offer.

'A book is what it is', Gauguin wrote of *Noa Noa*, '... incomplete, good ... however, if by telling a few stories you can express everything you want to say or to hint at, that is a great deal.'[9] This comment throws light on the nature of *Noa Noa*'s perfume, especially in its equation of 'to say' and 'to hint at': statement and allusion. It is a noteworthy coincidence that when Picasso was asked about the reality in Cubist painting, he said that it was 'not a reality you can take in your hand. It's more like a perfume – in front of you, behind you, to the sides. The scent is everywhere, but you don't quite know where it comes from.'[10]

Such a notion of the perfume of reality is a most apt model for the fragrance of *Noa Noa*. It carries an appropriate sense of something that is highly concentrated but unstable. It comes close too to Mallarmé's comment on Gauguin: 'It is extraordinary to be able to combine so much mystery with such explosive brilliance', a comment that Gauguin liked enough to repeat.[11] It is in the light of such a paradoxical blending that we might best look to understand *Noa Noa*'s relationship to the paintings it set out to explain, not least the obliqueness of evocation that it shares with them.

A brief consideration of Gauguin's illustrations in the Louvre MS may also offer some clues. It has already been mentioned that only a dozen or so of them were made at the same time as the text was copied out. The more or less arbitrary placing of the remainder, pasted into blank or flawed pages, has prompted writers to suggest that *all* of the illustrations were so placed.[12] Two at least of the original illustrations bear an explicit relationship to their placing: the 'title-page' already mentioned and the watercolour of Vairaoumati (Plate 101), whose adjacent text reads 'several weeks afterwards, Vairaoumati warned Oro that she was pregnant'.[13] In other cases, there is a reasonably arguable relevance. For instance, the episode in which a village elder counsels the natives to build better houses against the rain[14] is illustrated with two pasted-in watercolours of substantial thatched buildings.[15]

Those cases where the relevance is less easily argued may be more instructive. Take the images on p. 75 of the Louvre MS (Plate 100). The upper image of a lovemaking couple is a watercolour directly on the page that is an almost exact transcription, detail for detail, size for size, of an image in *Ancien Culte Mahorie*. It is unusual because figures in Gauguin's paintings seldom touch each other, let alone embrace. It is an image of great charm, both in its guilt-free simplicity and in the translucent bloom of its colour. The lower image is a trimmed print of an 1893/4 woodcut, pasted onto the page.[16] A version of *Manao Tupapau* – almost a Europeanized (i.e. 'corrupted') version in its enclosure and self-concealment – it poses a complete contrast to the image above, in form, mood and meaning. The text at this point is at the beginning of the wood-cutting expedition. We are told of the Maori youth's naïve questioning of Gauguin about lovemaking after which he says that Gauguin is not like other men.[17] The Louvre MS reads: 'I believe that Jotéfa is the first man in the world who has used that language to me – the language of a child, because one must be a child, is it not so, to imagine that an artist knows something of use . . .'[18]

The upper image is one of innocence, the lower of a grown woman in a foetal position. The relevance of these images to the talk of lovemaking, to childlike innocent intuitions and to the ever-present contrast between that sort of naïve clarity and the soiled condition of civilized thought is clear enough. The radiant combination of eroticism and innocence in the lovemaking image and its contrast with the opaque gloom and inertia of the other also anticipate the confusion of feelings that Gauguin tries to express later in the incident, involving shades of innocence, love, lust and shame. Finally, the placing of the couple inside the extravagant heraldic leaf, as if they were the flower, may be related to the story's theme of primitive man's oneness with nature, as well as to the theme of fragrance, *Noa Noa*.

Such a reading of the images comes very close to the empirical character of Gauguin's symbolism at large, which is personal and intuitive, equating the autobiographical with the universal, fact with fantasy, clarity with mystery. It is in this sense of a parallel, a literary and visual equivalent to his paintings, that *Noa Noa* may be understood as 'explanation' of them.

Gauguin's contribution to *Noa Noa* is a compendium of the experiences behind his paintings: principally, his encounters with Tahitian life, with the Tahitian landscape and with Maori mythology – all of them filtered through the imagination that they have also helped to form. In his *Cahier pour Aline*, in the context of Edgar Allan Poe, Gauguin wrote of 'the reproduction of what one may sense from outer nature but realized with the inner vision of the soul', also that 'the senses sometimes experience too little; they always experience too much.'[19] The literary techniques with which Gauguin presents these filtered experiences are also in many ways complementary to his paintings.

Gauguin twice characterized his writings as '. . . without sequence, like dreams, like all of life, made of fragments . . .'.[20] Of all his writings, the final form of *Noa Noa* has the clearest sense of structure, having both a semblance of chronology through the narrations and the pattern of alternation with Morice. Nevertheless, it retains something of the antipathy that Gauguin felt towards anything systematic or precise. In the Draft MS particularly, there is a familiar character of an assemblage of very concentrated, abrupt fragments: particles in a rather fluid parent body. The fragments of structure that we do find – his devices of re-use, repetition, symmetry; and his sense of caricature and silhouette – are common to his visual and verbal manners.

Morice wrote thoughtfully on Gauguin's repetition of motifs. 'Gauguin did not go [to Tahiti] seeking to revive his spirits by "new" subject matter. More than anyone perhaps, he was content with the same place or the same face, from which he knew how to recreate every time a transposition that was new, unseen-before.'[21] Strindberg's idea of Gauguin as 'the child who takes his toys apart to make new ones'[22] is more shrewd, not just because it coincides with the idea of the primitive as child, but also because Gauguin's literary and pictorial devices often have childlike qualities. Is it fortuitous that the titles of his three major original manuscripts are all alliterative: *Noa Noa, Racontars de Rapin, Avant et Après*? *Avant et Après* is sub-titled 'all this and all that', and in *Racontars de Rapin* we find 'my words wish to say this, but they also say that'.[23] There is a childlike insistence too in the endless repetition of his refrain *'ceci n'est pas un livre'* throughout *Avant et Après*. These playful instincts for repetition and for a symmetry that often involves paradox are paralleled by his eye for silhouette and for visual and verbal puns. There are two striking examples in the Draft MS: the sphinx-like rock on the sea-shore at Papeete, and the 'diseased coconut palm' that 'looked like a huge parrot'.[24] His drawings are alive with such an instinct: consider, for instance, the charged caricatural energy of his self-portrait cameo of 1888 (Plate 60), or the Breton drawing of cows in a landscape (right), where one of the pollarded willows takes on a silhouette remarkably like his own unmistakable profile. His brilliant perception of things seen was a crucial resource, for all his bullying talk of the poverty of an art based on nature. His Tahitian sketchbook is the journal of a visually very alert observer.

The visual motifs that he re-uses are mostly borrowed ready-made from other art – Field has assembled a most impressive range for the first Tahitian period[25] – and Gauguin is quite happy to quote repeatedly from other writers too – Poe, Voltaire, etc. – as well as from his own writing. Other repeated motifs relate to first-hand experience and to the filtering of that experience. One such is the silence of the Tahitian night. This motif occurs first in his Parisian dreams of what Tahiti will be. 'There in Tahiti, in the silence of the beautiful tropical night, I can listen to the sweet murmuring music of my heart, beating in loving harmony with the mysterious beings of my environment. Free at last . . .'[26] Other writers on Tahiti comment on the same phenomenon – Lafarge for instance[27] – and presumably Gauguin had read about it. In his second letter from Tahiti, the dream had become 'reality'. 'The night silence is even stronger than anything else. It can be felt; it is unbroken by even the cry of a bird . . . Nothing but this silence . . . I apprehend all the things that are going to invade my being and feel most amazingly at peace at this moment. It seems to me as if the turmoil in Europe exists no longer . . .'[28]

Back in France he wrote in the Draft MS: 'Silence of a Tahitian night. Only the beating of my heart could be heard . . . the moonlight filtering through like music . . . But silent . . . My hut was space, Freedom.'[29] In Tahiti the second time, he returned to the motif: 'Here near my hut, in complete silence, I dream of violent harmonies in the natural scents which intoxicate me . . . And comes the night when all things are at rest. My eyes close in order to see without comprehending the dream in infinite space stretching out before me, and I have the sensation of the melancholy progress of my hopes.'[30] The proliferation of poetic allusion and the gradual change of mood of the image are again like the shifts and nuances of a single fragrant sensation.

We know that Gauguin gave at least one reading from *Noa Noa* in his Paris studio.[31]

102 Cows in a landscape. *c.*1889. Watercolour, 26.5 × 32 cm. W343bis. Coll. S. Kramarsky, New York

One recent writer has made the thoughtful suggestion that maybe we should hear *Noa Noa* rather than read it. Her reasoning implies that we would then experience it in a mythic oral tradition like the Maoris, uninhibited by real chronological time.[32] It is also a sympathetic idea because sound has qualities in common with perfume that are lost on the printed page.

In face of the uncertainty of much surviving evidence, what conclusions about *Noa Noa* may in the end be possible? The conclusion that has virtually established itself as traditional is clearly unsatisfactory. According to this view the successive versions of *Noa Noa* were each less worthy of our attention because they were increasingly distant from the intention of the artist; in effect, the Draft MS alone is of lasting significance. A

103 *Self-portrait*. s. & d. 1889. Oil on wood, 79 × 52 cm. W323. National Gallery, Washington

quite contrary view seems to be more tenable; this recognizes that the Draft MS anticipates, even precipitates, much of what is to follow in later versions. If the clouds of prejudice do lift, it may be acknowledged that the final form published in 1901 more or less corresponds to Gauguin's first intention. The path towards such a clearer view of *Noa Noa* lies not in the isolation of its various forms, but in consideration of them all, together.

Gauguin's writing as a whole furnishes a very complete portrait of the man; the idea of *Noa Noa* is at its centre. He wrote of his last manuscript, *Avant et Après*, in similar terms: 'not in the least a literary work, something quite different: civilized man and the barbarian face to face'.[33] In one of his last letters to Charles Morice,[34] Gauguin reflected: 'As a painter Puvis de Chavannes is a scholar and not a man of letters, while I myself am not a scholar, but maybe I am a man of letters.'

Notes

1 *Écho de Paris*, May 13th, 1895. trans. Danielsson, 1966, p. 184.
2 p. 13. See also Note 12, p. 67.
3 pp. 28, 37.
4 *Avant et Après*, p. 1.
5 Segalen, *Lettres*, 1950, p. 56.
6 Field, 1977, p. 43.
7 Malingue, *Letters*, 1948, p. 146.
8 O. Mirbeau, 'Retour de Tahiti', *Écho de Paris*, November 14th, 1893. Cutting in *Cahier pour Aline*, n.p.
9 Malingue, *Letters*, 1948, p. 214.
10 Quoted in D. Ashton (ed.), *Picasso on Art*, New York, 1972, p. 155.
11 Louvre MS, p. 3.
12 e.g. Huyghe 1951; Loize, 1966.
13 Louvre MS, p. 157.
14 Chapter III of Draft MS.
15 Louvre MS, p. 71.
16 See Guérin, 1927, No. 38.
17 See p. 25.
18 Louvre MS, pp. 74–7.
19 *Cahier pour Aline*, n.p.
20 ibid and *Avant et Après*.
21 Morice, 1920, p. 186.
22 *Avant et Après*, p. 21.
23 *Racontars de Rapin*, p. 17.
24 p. 17.
25 Field, 1977.
26 Malingue, *Letters*, 1948, p. 137.
27 Lafarge, 1914. See Note 26, p.70
28 Malingue, *Letters*, 1948, p. 163.
29 p. 17.
30 Malingue, *Letters*, 1948, p. 216.
31 Rotonchamp, 1906, p. 129.
32 Teilhet-Fisk, 1983, p. 181 n.5.
33 Malingue, *Letters*, 1948, p. 232.
34 ibid, p. 227.

Correspondence between the Draft MS and the Louvre MS

(This relates the contents and sequence of the version of *Noa Noa* that Gauguin wrote to the collaborative version that he approved)

DRAFT MS		LOUVRE MS
		'Memory and Imagination' (Morice's preface)
		Chapter I (pp. 3–25)
		Songeries (prose by Morice)
I	Arrival in Papeete; funeral of Pomaré V; moves to Mataiea; Titi.	**Chapter II** (pp. 26–47)
		Le Conteur Parle
II	Sea-shore at night; man with an axe; the painting of *Vahine no te Tiare*.	(adding the Story of Princess Vaïtua, between the accounts of Titi and the sea-shore at night)
		Chapter III (pp. 48–65)
		Vivo (poems by Morice, partly added later)
		(pp. 55–65 filled with illustrations)
		Chapter IV (pp. 67–89)
		Le Conteur Parle
III	Alone again; the 'parable' of the old man.	
IV	'Civilization leaves me'; the wood-cutting expedition.	
V	The story of *Pape Moë*.	
		Chapter V (pp. 89–96)
		Pape Moë (poem by Morice, added later)
		(pp. 93–6 blank)

DRAFT MS		LOUVRE MS
		Chapter VI (pp. 97–116)
		Le Conteur Parle
VI	Journey around the island; *Hina Maruru*; meeting with Tehamana in Taravao.	
VII	Life with Tehamana in Mataiea; Legend of Roua; *Manao Tupapau*.	(omits Legend of Roua – moved to Chapter VIII)
VIII	The story of the wedding.	(adds the Story of the Ear-rings, after *Manao Tupapau*)
		Chapter VII (pp. 117–27)
		Parahi te Marae (poems by Morice)
		(pp. 124–7 filled with illustrations)
		Chapter VIII (pp. 129–67)
		Le Conteur Parle
		'La Génèse Polynésienne' (from *Ancien Culte Mahorie*, but adds the Story of the Grotto of Mara)
		Chapter IX (pp. 169–89)
		Nave Nave Fenua (prose and verse by Morice 'to come')
		(pp. 171–89 filled with illustrations)
		Chapter X (pp. 191–201)
		Le Conteur Parle
IX	The tunny-fishing expedition; legend of Rouahatou; Tehamana's prayer.	
		Chapter XI (pp. 203–4)
		Le Conteur achève son récit
X	The departure for France.	
	Appendix – 'The dirty truth' (omitted from Louvre MS).	

Chronology of Noa Noa

1891–3   Gauguin's first stay in Tahiti.

           Gauguin takes notes from *Voyages aux Îles du Grand Océan* (1837) by J. A. Moerenhout and copies them into his *Ancien Culte Mahorie* notebook, which he illustrates with watercolour drawings.

1893   Gauguin returns to Paris.

           Before or after consultations with Charles Morice, Gauguin drafts his first manuscript for *Noa Noa* (Draft MS), from which Morice works on a revised version; three further narrative episodes (see pp. 49–57) are also drafted at this time. The text of the book is to be divided more or less equally between Gauguin's narratives and Morice's poetry.

1893/5?   Gauguin copies out Morice's revision of the narrative chapters and those parts of Morice's own contribution that are completed. This includes a whole chapter on Maori mythology taken straight from *Ancien Culte Mahorie*. This version is the Louvre MS.

1894   Gauguin makes a series of ten large woodcuts related to *Noa Noa*.

1895   Gauguin returns to Tahiti.

           He takes with him the Louvre MS. Probably he leaves with Morice the *Ancien Culte Mahorie* MS, as well as his Draft MS.

1895–7   Morice completes his own contributions to *Noa Noa* and makes some further editorial adjustment to Gauguin's texts.

c. 1896/8   Gauguin adds an 'appendix' to the Louvre MS, entitled *Diverses Choses*, a miscellany of notes on painting, religion, marriage, etc., with some *collé* illustrations. At around the same time, he fills up with illustrations the pages of the album left blank for poems by Morice that never arrive.

1897   Excerpts from *Noa Noa* are published in two issues of the journal *La Revue Blanche*: October 15th; November 1st. All of Gauguin's texts appear. Gauguin receives the first issue and copies into the Louvre MS two poems by Morice that are new to him. Probably he never sees the second issue.

1901   *Noa Noa*, Éditions de la Plume, Paris.

           This is the first and only complete edition of *Noa Noa* to be published, incorporating all of Morice's material. It is published under their two names at Morice's expense. Probably Gauguin does not see a copy.

           Gauguin leaves Tahiti for the Marquesas Islands.

1903   Death of Gauguin.

           The Louvre MS is inherited by Daniel de Monfried.

1908   Morice sells Gauguin's Draft MS to a print dealer in Paris.

1910   Extracts from the Louvre MS are published for the first time, in the journal *Les Marges*, Paris.

1919   Death of Morice.

First English translation of *Noa Noa* published, Nicholas Brown, New York. The translation by O. F. Theis is of Gauguin's texts only, taken either from the excerpts in *La Revue Blanche* or from the 1901 edition.

1924   *Noa Noa, Voyage de Tahiti*, Crès, Paris.

First publication of the text of the Louvre MS, illustrated with woodcuts by de Monfried, after Gauguin's paintings. De Monfried donates the Louvre MS to the Louvre in 1925.

1926   A facsimile edition of the Louvre MS is published by Ganymed, Berlin.

1951   A facsimile edition of *Ancien Culte Mahorie* is published. René Huyghe's text makes clear the borrowings from Moerenhout within *Noa Noa*.

1954   First publication of Gauguin's Draft MS, in facsimile, by Sagot–Le Garrec, Paris.

1961   First English translation of the Draft MS published as *Noa Noa, Voyage to Tahiti*, Bruno Cassirer, Oxford. The translation by Jonathan Griffin has an important critical 'Postscript' by Jean Loize.

1966   First French edition of the Draft MS is published in Jean Loize's *Noa Noa par Paul Gauguin*, Balland/SPADEM, Paris.

Bibliography

I   Editions of *Noa Noa* (A more exhaustive list may be found in Loize 1966)

Noa Noa (Excerpts), *La Revue Blanche*, Paris, Vol. XIV, 1897. No. 105, Oct. 15th, pp. 81–103; No. 106, Nov. 1st, pp. 166–90

Noa Noa, Éditions de la Plume, Paris, 1901

Noa Noa (Excerpts from the Louvre MS), *Les Marges*, Paris, No. 21, May 1910, pp. 169–74

Noa Noa, Nicholas Brown, New York, 1919 (trans. O. F. Theis). (First English translation; excerpts from 1897 or 1901 editions)

Noa Noa. Voyage de Tahiti, G. Crès, Paris, 1924. Text of Louvre MS. Illustrated by D. de Monfried

Noa Noa, Ganymed, Berlin, 1926. Facsimile of the Louvre MS

Noa Noa, Voyage à Tahiti, Jan Forlag, Stockholm, 1947. Reproduction of the Louvre MS

Noa Noa, Sagot–Le Garrec, Paris, 1954. Facsimile of the Draft MS

Noa Noa, Bruno Cassirer, Oxford, 1961 (trans. J. Griffin). (First English translation of the Draft MS). Postscript by J. Loize

Noa Noa par Paul Gauguin by Jean Loize, André Balland, Paris, 1966. (First French edition of the Draft MS)

II   Other writings by Gauguin

Notes Synthétiques (*c.* 1884–8). Ten unnumbered pages of a carnet used in Rouen, Copenhagen, Paris and Brittany during 1884–8. Facsimile edition, Hammer Galleries, New York, 1961. Texts, R. Cogniat and J. Rewald

Ancien Culte Mahorie (*c.* 1892–3). Cabinet des Dessins, Louvre, Paris. (Moreau–Nélaton Bequest). Facsimile edition, La Palme, Paris, 1951. Text, R. Huyghe

Cahier pour Aline (1893). Fondation Jacques Doucet, University of Paris. Facsimile edition, Société des Amis de la Bibliothéque d'Art et d'Archéologie de l'Université de Paris, 1963. Text, S. Damiron

Racontars de Rapin (1902). Falaize, Paris, 1951

Avant et Après (1903). Facsimile edition, Kurt Wolff, Leipzig, 1918. Trans. *Paul Gauguin's Intimate Journals*, Van Wyck Brooks, 1923

Oviri, Écrits d'Un Sauvage (ed. M. Guérin). Gallimard, Paris, 1974. Trans. *The Writings of a Savage* (Introduction by W. Andersen), New York, 1978. (This anthology of Gauguin texts includes an edited translation of the Draft MS of *Noa Noa* and excerpts from the *Diverses Choses* of the Louvre MS)

III   Correspondence

A complete edition of Gauguin correspondence is in preparation. The editions listed here include the most recent collections of letters in English and French

Letters of Paul Gauguin to Georges-Daniel de Monfried, Heinemann, London, 1923. Trans. R. Pielkovo. Text, F. O'Brien

Paul Gauguin, Lettres à sa Femme et ses Amis, Grasset, Paris, 1946. Trans. H. Stenning, Saturn, London n.d. (1948). Text, M. Malingue

Lettres de Gauguin à Daniel de Monfried, Falaize, Paris, 1950. Ed. Mme A. Joly-Segalen. Text, V. Segalen

Bibliography

IV   Relevant texts

J. A. Moerenhout: *Voyages aux Îles du Grand Océan*, 2 vols, Paris, 1837. Reprinted 1942

M. E. Bovis: *État de la Société Tahitienne à l'Arrivée des Européens. Revue Coloniale*, 1855. Reprinted, Papeete, 1909

C. Morice: *La Littérature de Tout à l'Heure*, Paris, 1889

H. Adams: *Tahiti (Memoirs of Arii Taimai; Memoirs of Marau Taaroa, Last Queen of Tahiti)*, 1893. Reprinted (ed. R. E. Spiller), New York, 1947

A. Johnstone: *Recollections of R. L. Stevenson in the Pacific*, London, 1905

J. de Rotonchamp: *Paul Gauguin 1848–1903*, Paris, 1906. New edition, Paris, 1925

J. Lafarge: *Reminiscences of the South Seas*, London, 1914

C. Morice: *Paul Gauguin*, Paris, 1919. New edition, Paris, 1920

R. Rey: *Gauguin*, Paris, 1924

M. Guérin: *L'Oeuvre Gravé de Gauguin*, 2 vols, Paris, 1927

E. Best: *Forest Lore of the Maori*, Wellington, 1942

H. Dorra: 'The First Eves in Gauguin's Eden', *Gazette des Beaux Arts*, Paris, XLI, 1953, pp. 189–202

J. Rewald: *Post Impressionism. From Van Gogh to Gauguin*, New York, 1956. Revised 1962

G. Wildenstein (ed.): *Gauguin. Sa Vie, Son Oeuvre. Documents Inédits*, Paris, 1958

H. Perruchot: *La Vie de Gauguin*, Paris, 1961. Trans. London, 1963, 1965

C. Gray: *Sculpture and Ceramics of Paul Gauguin*, Baltimore, 1963

M. Bodelsen: *Gauguin's Ceramics,* London, 1964

G. Wildenstein: *Paul Gauguin. I. Catalogue*, Paris, 1964

B. Danielsson: *Gauguin in the South Seas*, New York, 1966

B. Danielsson & P. O'Reilly: *Gauguin. Journaliste à Tahiti & ses articles des 'Guêpes'*, Paris, 1966

W. Davenport, B. Danielsson, R. Field: *Gauguin and Exotic Art*, Pennsylvania, 1969

W. Andersen: *Gauguin's Paradise Lost*, New York, 1971

H. R. Rookmaaker: *Gauguin and 19th Century Art Theory*, Amsterdam, 1972

S. Phelps: *Art and Artefacts of the Pacific . . . The Hooper Collection*, London, 1976

R. Field: *Paul Gauguin. The Paintings of the First Voyage to Tahiti*, New York, 1977

N. Wadley: *Gauguin*, Oxford, 1978

T. Salmon, H. Adams: *Lettres de Tahiti*, Papeete, 1980

J. Teilhet-Fisk: *Paradise Reviewed. An Interpretation of Gauguin's Polynesian Symbolism*, Michigan, 1983

List of illustrations

The author and John Calmann and Cooper Ltd would like to thank the owners of the various works for permission to reproduce them in this book. Photographs are from the museum or collection indicated below, unless otherwise stated.

Particular thanks are due to the photographic service of the Réunion des Musées Nationaux, Paris, which arranged for the photography of the various manuscript pages.

1   *Noa Noa* (Fragrant). *c.*1894. Colour woodcut on end-grain boxwood with stencils, 35 × 20cm. Guérin 17. Museum of Modern Art, New York (Lillie P. Bliss Coll.)
2   Still life (after Delacroix). 1894/7. Watercolour, 17 × 12cm. Frontispiece of the Louvre MS
3   *Ta Matete* (We shall not go to market today). s. & d. 1892. 73 × 92cm. W476. Kunstmuseum, Basel (photo Hinz)
4   *L'Univers est Créé* (The universe was created). *c.*1894/5. Woodcut, 20.5 × 35.5cm. Guérin 25-6. Nationalmuseum, Stockholm (photo Statens Konstmuseer)
5   *Man with an Axe.* s. & d. 1891. 92 × 69cm. W430. Coll. Mr and Mrs Alexander M. Lewyt, New York
6   Crested head. *c.*1893. Pen and ink, 3.5 × 3.5cm. Draft MS, supplement to p.7
7   'Taoa'. *c.*1891/3. Pen and ink over pencil, 10.5 × 7.5cm. Carnet de Tahiti, p.43
8   *Vahine no te Tiare* (Woman with a flower). s. & d. 1891. 70 × 46cm. W420. Ny Carlsberg Glyptotek, Copenhagen
9   *Te Raau Rahi* (The big tree). s. & d. 1891. 71.5 × 91.5cm. W437. Cleveland Museum of Art (jointly owned by the Museum and an anonymous collector)
10 Palm trees and horse. *c.*1891/3. Pencil, 16.5 × 11cm. Carnet de Tahiti, p.39
11 *Tahitian Village.* s. & d. 1892. 90 × 70cm. W480. Ny Carlsberg Glyptotek, Copenhagen
12 Illustration to the woodcutting expedition. *c.*1894/5. Pen and watercolour, 9.5 × 19.5cm. Louvre MS, p.79
13 *Te Fare Hymenee* (The house of song). s. & d. 1892. 50 × 90cm. W477. Baltimore Museum of Art (photo Courtauld Institute, London)
14 *Pape Moë* (Mysterious water). s. & d. 1893. 99 × 75cm. W498. Bührle Collection, Zürich
15 Landscape. *c.*1896/7? Watercolour, 19.5 × 28cm. Louvre MS, p.183
16 *Manao Tupapau* (The spirit of the dead watches/ She thinks of the spirit of the dead). s. & d. 1892. 73 × 92cm. W457. Albright-Knox Art Gallery, Buffalo (A. Conger Goodyear Coll., 1965)
17 River. *c.*1893. Pen and ink, 3 × 2.5cm. Draft MS, p.16
18 Maori spirit. *c.*1894/5. Pen and watercolour, 5 × 6cm. Louvre MS, p.73
19 Illustration to 'Birth of the Stars'. *c.*1892. Pen and watercolour, 10 × 16cm. Ancien Culte Mahorie MS, p.42
20 Illustration to the legend of Rouahatou. *c.*1892. Pen and watercolour, 7 × 15cm. Ancien Culte Mahorie MS, p.36
21 Illustration to 'Birth of the Stars'. *c.*1892. Pen and watercolour, 15 × 16cm. Ancien Culte Mahorie MS, p.40
22 Sailing boat. *c.*1896/7. Pen and watercolour, 17 × 12cm. Louvre MS, p.187
23 Studies. *c.*1891/3. Pencil and watercolour, 16.5 × 11cm. Carnet de Tahiti, p.12
24 *Hina. c.*1891/3. Tamanu wood and painted gilt, 37 × 13.4 × 10.8cm. Gray 95. Hirshhorn Museum and Sculpture Garden, Smithsonian Institution, Washington (Museum purchase with funds provided under the Institution's Collections Acquisitions Program, 1981)
25 Fishing boat. *c.*1893. Pen and ink, 3 × 12cm. Draft MS, p.24
26 Horned head. Photograph of a lost sculpture. Gray A-13. Louvre MS, p.56
27 *Hina Tefatou* (also called The Moon and the Earth). s. & d. 1893. 112 × 62cm. W499. Museum of Modern Art, New York (Lillie P. Bliss Coll.)
28 *Parau na te varua Ino* (Words of the Devil). s. & d. 1892. 94 × 70cm. W458. National Gallery, Washington
29 *Vairaoumati Tei Oa* (Her name is Vairaoumati). s. & d. 1892. 91 × 60cm. W450. Hermitage, Leningrad

List of illustrations

Index

159

Index